SUPERGOAL

With BILLY ZEOLI

H   11

/5

Fleming H. Revell Company
Old Tappan, New Jersey

Scripture references in this volume are from the *King James Version of the Bible* unless otherwise identified.

Scripture references identified LB are from *The Living Bible* by Kenneth N. Taylor © copyright 1971, and are used by permission of the publisher, Tyndale House Publishers.

The material in "God's Game Plan," © 1972 Billy Zeoli, appeared in *Decision* magazine, October 1972.

796.33
Z

Library of Congress Cataloging in Publication Data

Zeoli, Billy.
　　Supergoal.

　　CONTENTS: Zeoli, B. Christianity and athletics.—
Landry, T. Leadership.—Dale, C. Winning. [etc.]
　　　1. Christian life—1960—　　2. Religion and sports.
I. Title.
BV4501.2.Z46　　　248'.42'0922　[B]　　　72–8552
ISBN 0–8007–0584–X

CONTENTS

PREFACE

The athletes in this book are representative of thousands of athletes in the high school, college and professional football ranks.

These men and their Christian lives are a direct result
   of the concern,
   of the prayers,
   of the love of many, many people.
These people are
   pastors who have taken time to pray and counsel.
   Sunday-school teachers who have helped point the way to Christ.
   God-loving mothers and fathers who lived the Christian life before these men—while these men were growing boys.
   other Christian athletes who have been faithful in presenting Christ—Buddy Dial, Don Schinnick, Raymond Berry, Bill Glass, Bill Wade.
   high-school and college coaches, who point young men in the right direction in their formative time in life.
Organizations that have worked and witnessed—

      Campus Crusade for Christ
      Fellowship of Christian Athletes
      Sport World Chaplaincy
      Teen Crusade
      Youth for Christ

Individuals who have taken time to organize and to
speak at countless chapel services for the football
teams in the NFL—

Sam Anderson	Bill Lewis
Sam Bender	Al Long
Ira Eshleman	Clebe McClary
Paul Eshleman	Bobby Richardson
Bob Harrington	Tom Skinner
Bill Krisher	Dave Swanson

Eddie Waxer

I personally would like to thank the board and staff of

Gospel Films

with whom I work,
who not only urged me to share the lives of these
athletes with you, but
who also have freed me to have a ministry among
professional football and baseball players.

My special thanks to Richard and Helen DeVos
who have given of themselves
and have given of their means
to make my sports ministry possible.

Also, I warmly and deeply thank the men in this book for
sharing themselves on paper, that it might enrich and help
us. It is their prayer
and it is my prayer
that this book will be used of God to help you realize that
you can find the complete balance of life,
not just physical and mental,
but spiritual as well,
in the person of Jesus Christ, our Saviour!

1

CHRISTIANITY AND ATHLETICS

BILLY ZEOLI

"Since we have such a huge crowd of men of faith watching us from the grandstands, let us strip off anything that slows us down or holds us back, and especially those sins that wrap themselves so tightly around our feet and trip us up; and let us run with patience the particular race that God has set before us" (Hebrews 12:1 LB).

"I want to suggest that you finish what you started to do a year ago, for you were not only the first to propose this idea, but the first to begin doing something about it. Having started the ball rolling so enthusiastically, you should carry this project through to completion just as gladly, giving whatever you can out of whatever you have. Let your enthusiastic idea at the start be equalled by your realistic action now" (2 Corinthians 8:10, 11 LB).

"So take a new grip with your tired hands, stand firm on your shaky legs, and mark out a straight, smooth path for your feet so that those who follow you, though weak and lame, will not fall and hurt themselves, but become strong" (Hebrews 12:12, 13 LB).

"In a race, everyone runs but only one person gets first prize. So run your race to win. To win the contest you must deny yourselves many things that would keep you from doing your best. An athlete goes to all this trouble just to win a blue ribbon or a silver cup, but we do it for a heavenly reward that never disappears. So I run straight to the goal with purpose in every step. I fight to win. I'm not just shadowboxing or playing around. Like an athlete I punish my body, treating it roughly, training it to do what it should, not what it wants to. Otherwise I fear that after enlisting others for the race, I myself might be declared unfit and ordered to stand aside" (1 Corinthians 9:24–27 LB).

"No, dear brothers, I am still not all I should be but I am bringing all my energies to bear on this one thing: Forgetting the past and looking forward to what lies ahead, I strain to reach the end of the race and receive the prize for which God is calling us up to heaven because of what Christ Jesus did for us" (Philippians 3:13, 14 LB).

What you have just read are passages from Scripture written by the Apostle Paul which compare the Christian life and athletics.

Christianity and athletics *do* go together.

The comparison of Christianity and athletics is an *obvious, natural* comparison.

The overall purpose of this book is to show that the Christian life of professional football players today and the problems which they face in life, on *and* off the football field, can be of help to us in our everyday experiences.

The athletes in these pages have written on important subjects concerning the Christian life.

> They have found God's game plan begins with the love of God and becomes personal when they put their faith in His Son.
>
> They have found that winning in the Christian life and being a success for God is a direct result of their courage and determination, coupled with the Holy Spirit's indwelling power.

These factors make them leaders for Christ.

Thus I have singled out these athletes to write on topics which they have lived. Some are shorter than others because some topics can be more easily handled in a shorter space.

Everyone is aware of

> the glamour,
> the adulation,
> the popularity,
> the national acclaim,

that goes with being a professional football player, but many people do not realize that the athlete's life holds a great deal of uncertainty.

At any given moment
> he can be injured—
> he can be out for the season—
> he can be replaced by someone else who can move him out of his position just by running one-tenth of one second faster.

An athlete's life can be changed with
> the cut of a squad—
> the decision of a coach—
> the bounce of a ball.

It is imperative that athletes have something tangible—something they can tie their lives to. These men you are hearing from in this book believe that this *something* is the living person of Jesus Christ!

There is a tremendous moving among athletes today by the Spirit of God.

It is a reality—*an exciting reality*—that ought to bring excitement to your soul as it has to mine. The realization of it should help us greatly in understanding how Christian athletes and their experiences can be of direct benefit to us in our lives *inwardly*.

Witness: Carroll Dale, Green Bay Packers. Carroll Dale knows what it means to win—

    to win a starting position.

    to win All-Pro honors.

    to win Super Bowls.

Yet he also learned that teams go through periods when injuries and problems cause them to lose. He has bared his soul to us that we might, in the Christian life, aim at *winning*, yet learn that *losing* is a vivid reality!

Witness: Jim Houston, Cleveland Browns. I remember when Jim Houston first accepted Christ as Saviour—

    he was so excited.

    he was so enthusiastic.

    he wanted so much to share.

In the locker room a few days later, he pulled Bill Glass to one side.

    JIM: Bill, tell some of the guys about the plan.

    BILL: What plan, Jim?

    JIM: God's plan. Tell them how they can come to know Jesus Christ as Saviour like you and I.

This beautiful enthusiasm for Christ is something that those of us who have been believers for years sometimes do not *feel,* do not *show.*

Witness: Bob Vogel, Baltimore Colts. As chapel leader of the Colts, Bob has a great heritage.

Don Shinnick started that chapel.

Raymond Berry (who Don introduced to Christ) then led the group.

Bob, with other players, now coordinates its outreach. This team not only has chapel services, but meets every Friday night—husbands and wives together—to study God's Word. Bob's emphasis is on the positive. He told me, "Bill, let's share the joy of Christ and give a positive reason for our faith in Christ."

Witness: Lem Barney, Detroit Lions. The first time I spoke for the Detroit Lions' chapel, Lem Barney took me to a table to have breakfast with some of the players. We were talking about Christ when the trainer came over to the table.

"Men, let's move. It's time to get taped."

The men gave him an ignoring wave and kept talking.

"Men, you've got to be taped—NOW!"

Charlie Sanders replied,

"Leave us alone. We can be taped later. We want to hear about Jesus Christ."

Witness: Norm Evans, Miami Dolphins. When I called Norm Evans and asked him to write the chapter on determination, the first thing he said was, "Billy, I'll call you back in a couple of days. I must pray about this."

Norm Evans prays about everything in his life: I mean

literally *everything!* Many Christians do this, BUT—for a
man to be that determined in his life and to be that determined about *God's* determination in his life, shows how
Christ can move into the area of a man's will—as well as a
man's heart.

Witness: Charley Harraway, Washington Redskins. Charley writes about love. In a time of injury, in a time when
he could not start this past season, in discouragement and
physical weakness, Charley showed the love of Christ by
his life and his attitude.

> These men don't beat the air.
> These men don't shadowbox.
> These men live Christ daily.

They are evidence, in the flesh, of the moving of the Spirit
of God among athletes today.

The Christian athlete has another significant lesson for
us. This one is OUTWARD, yet a direct result of the in-
ward work of Christ. Football gives Christian men a chance
to express and share Christ on a personal basis in two ways.

1. On a personal, one-to-one basis with their teammates.
2. On a great platform, telling others about Jesus
   Christ.

Because of the national platform and prestige of the game,
because of who they are as football players, *because* of
their accomplishments on the field, football gives them this
great platform to tell others about Jesus Christ and brings
into great focus the personal lives they lead, on *and* off
the field.

Tom Landry and Roger Staubach are two superb examples of what I mean.

More people watched Super Bowl VI than any other television event in history. There were tremendous Christians on both the Miami Dolphins and the Dallas Cowboys. When the game was over and Tom Landry was lifted onto the shoulders of the Cowboys, the world suddenly realized that Tom Landry, after years of frustration, was the "winningest" coach in pro football and now had won the biggest event in sports—THE SUPER BOWL!

When Tom Landry now speaks about football, everyone listens.

When Tom Landry now says that the most important things in his life are

> Jesus Christ,
> his family
> and football,

in that order, men of all ages start reassessing the personal motivations and goals of their own lives.

In Roger Staubach's home, I saw more trophies than some *teams* have in their trophy cases. I was overwhelmed with all that Roger had won. He said, "Billy, next year I could end up being a bum. This year I am a hero. These trophies *do* mean something, but

> Christianity is the center of my life and my home.

What means the most to me is that I am a Christian. When my football career is over, it is my Christian principles which will carry me through my life."

When interviewed by the national press, Roger said,

> "Christianity is my life—football is my occupation."

Sports are a common denominator among most men.
Whether these men be

> college graduates,
> high school drop-outs,
> factory workers,
> company executives—

whether they are

> Protestant
> Catholic
> Jewish—

whether they are

> black or
> white—

on Sunday afternoon *millions* of them are glued to television sets watching professional football.

Because of the national prominence of men like
Roger Staubach and Tom Landry
and the other men in this book;
because of the sports common denominator factor,
people are listening to what they have to say.

Let me take time out to tell you about that part of the
Sunday ball game that you never see. There are now about
twenty teams (out of twenty-six teams in the National
Football League) that hold chapel services before their
games.

That's right—twenty out of twenty-six!

Such was not always the case. I remember the first chapel
service I spoke for. Bill Glass invited me to speak to the

Cleveland Browns about ten years ago. I traveled all the way from Grand Rapids, Michigan, to Cleveland, Ohio, and ended up speaking to three players! One of them was Bill Glass.

I contrast that time with the game between Baltimore and Miami for the AFC-1971 championship and the game between San Francisco and Dallas for the NFC-1971 championship. On that Sunday morning, **ALL FOUR** of the teams had chapel services. There were over thirty (out of forty) players in attendance at the Dallas Cowboy service, with all the coaches in attendance, as well. Baltimore, Miami, and San Francisco services were also well attended.

Many of you will never have a chance to attend professional football chapel services. These are some of the most thrilling experiences in my life. Sunday starts early for professional football players. Some have such nervous energy that they are up and walking at 5 A.M. Professional football teams always eat four hours prior to game time. Their breakfasts are the kind we would never turn down— steak and eggs. It is interesting to watch a 275-pound tackle—so intent on the coming game—walk into this breakfast.

He cuts a piece of steak (and only one),
    puts it into his mouth,
        chews it,
           and leaves.

He is totally oblivious to what he has done! It is equally interesting to watch a little cornerback, 175-pounds, put away *two* steaks. Every man is different from all the others.

        Some players are extremely quiet.
        Some are openly edgy.

Some are tremendously superstitious.
Some cover their anxiety by laughing.

All realize that the entire week's work is wrapped up in that sixty minutes on the field that afternoon.

Our chapel services are held just before breakfast.
Most of the men arrive early.
Many read the sports page.
Some sit and stare.
Some cheer you on with, "Don't preach the same old sermon, Z!"
Some bring their Bibles.
Their voices range from a southern twang—to a Harvard accent.
Most are dressed casually yet stylishly.
These are intelligent men—over 90 percent are college graduates.
Their football playbooks contain as many as a thousand plays.
They have come because they want to.
They listen intently to the message, as intently as they play on the field.
They remember well.
They repeat and review when questioned.
These are highly disciplined men:
when asked to pray, they quickly bow their heads;
when we read the Word of God, they uniformly stand to their feet.
They are open.
They are receptive.
The sermon is given.

The final prayer is made.

The opportunity to make a decision is presented. Often men make decisions for Christ.

When a player makes a decision for Christ, I try to follow him up with personal counseling and give him a Bible as well as printed material. When the chapel service is over, I go along with the men to breakfast and utilize the remaining time sharing Christ.

I hope through the lives and the words of the men in this book, YOU will be able to comprehend that which the Apostle Paul shared with us—

THE COMPARISON OF THE CHRISTIAN LIFE AND THE LIFE OF ATHLETICS

The closing chapter of this book is a message I have used with every football team to which I have spoken. It is the Gospel of Jesus Christ.

It is the Message that has

> transformed,
> changed,
> revitalized

the lives of every one of us in this book.

The goal of every professional football player is to win the Super Bowl.

Our goal for you, HIGH SCHOOL AND COLLEGE STUDENTS—

You might never make the big leagues in pro football, but you can make the big leagues in life by utilizing your life to witness for Jesus Christ, whether on the football field or in the chemistry lab.

Our goal for you, BUSINESSMAN—

It is too late for you to be a ball player, but just like these athletes have done, you can share your faith in Christ with the world that is around you, with those in your sphere of influence.

Our goal for you, GIRLS AND WOMEN—

Whether you understand the game of football or not, the goal is for you to apply these spiritual challenges in your own areas of life.

Again: The goal of every professional football player is to win the Super Bowl,

but the men in this book have an additional goal—
the Supergoal—

accepting Jesus Christ as Saviour and letting the life and love of Christ live through them.

This goal can be yours, as well!

Tom Landry

Tom Landry   Head Coach   Dallas Cowboys

Tom began his second decade with the Dallas Cowboys in 1970. Since 1965 his team has won five divisional titles and twice was on the brink of going to the Super Bowl, losing by narrow margins to Green Bay. In 1971 they went all the way, beating Miami in Super Bowl VI in New Orleans.

A native of Texas, Tom played college football at the University of Texas on Longhorn teams which went to the Sugar Bowl in 1948 and the Orange Bowl in 1949.

He played halfback for New York from 1950 to 1953 and was a player-coach in 1954–55. In 1954, he was named All-Pro. In 1956 he retired as a player and in his first year as full-time coach, the Giants won the world championship.

Tom and his wife, Alicia, live in Dallas the year round. They have three children, Tom, Jr., Kitty, and Lisa.

TOM LANDRY
DALLAS COWBOYS—HEAD COACH

I've been with Tom Landry in both victory and defeat.
I've been with him
> on the day when he won the Super Bowl—
> on the day when he lost the Super Bowl.

Although his outward appearance and his feeling about
each game was different, he was the same consistent
Christian. I have observed his life from very close up.

> The people around him,
> the people who know him best,

are amazed at his ability to demonstrate consistently, by
his life and his talk, the gospel of Jesus Christ.

In the years that Tom Landry has been my friend, I
have never asked him to do something that he has not done
with a warm and gracious spirit. Tom has been an example to me

> of discipline and
> of love.

The coach's job is to win. This, Tom Landry does very well.
But behind that winning spirit is a love and concern for
people. Before one of the biggest games of Tom's career,
my six-year-old son David sent Tom Landry a little piece
of paper

> made in the shape of a cross

and said to me, "Daddy, have Tom Landry carry that in
his pocket." I gave it to Tom and he smiled and I forgot all
about it.

In the locker room right after winning the Super Bowl,
Tom reached into his pocket. He gave me the piece of

paper and said to me, "Thank David for letting me carry this for him."

In his first season as head coach in Dallas, Tom lost eleven games and tied one. Last season, his team won the world championship—the Super Bowl. I can think of no one better suited to write about

LEADERSHIP

than a man who has been at the bottom, and *through God's strength* and his own *God-given ability,* has come to the top.

Recently we made a film about Tom Landry. Our real problem was NOT in trying to find people who would give us testimony about his ability as a leader and his Christian stand, BUT in trying to select from so much material. Most people who know football, coaches and players alike, will tell you that Tom Landry is

a leader among leaders.

The same is unquestionably true in his Christian life. Tom Landry is

a Christian among Christians.

2

LEADERSHIP

TOM LANDRY

As a pro football coach, I'm always looking for men with leadership ability, or the potential for leadership. I really never sat down and outlined what I think leadership is, but there isn't any question that we can identify it in people.

Although I've heard it said that this person or that player or that coach is a born leader, I don't believe that leaders are born. I believe that they are developed, that leadership can be created. If a person seems to be a born leader, all that we're really saying is that he has developed the characteristics that make leaders, without having actually been conscious of the fact that he was developing them.

People have always told me that a leader is someone who has power and I guess that's right. What makes a leader? I don't know the answer to that. You can look at one quarterback and you know he can lead people. Then you look at another quarterback, with the same great talents, and he may not be able to lead anybody. I don't know how to explain it but you get a good feeling when you're around somebody who can lead because you know you can have confidence in him. You know he's going to get you where you want to go, and I guess that's really what being a leader is all about.

I believe that a leader must be a doer, although not necessarily a star. I think he must be willing to pay the price—to sacrifice and do the things that are necessary to be successful in his field.

I think one of the most important things in becoming a leader is to get very good at your position. Once a person is accomplished in skills he reaches a point where he's confident, himself. When we have a whole team of skilled players, they develop confidence in each other and this tends to build a winning spirit. You must have confidence in everybody who plays with you, confidence that he can do his job, that he is skilled and dedicated. Once you've accomplished this, you begin to develop the spirit that helps you win.

Discipline is very important to winning. You can't have a real winning team without it. In fact, I don't think you can have a successful life without it. I feel very strongly about this, and I think that most other coaches do, too. When you're disciplined, it means you're able to pay the price, as we say in our game. You're able to sacrifice things that may be easier to do in order to do the things that will bring success. I think this is very important, both in football and in a Christian's life. I think this is where football and Christianity have a very close relationship, because to live a Christian life a person has to be just as disciplined in the things he does as a player does to be successful in football. We feel that we can build character and develop good traits in athletes and this is why I think an athlete is such a great candidate for Jesus Christ.

Many people ask me how my Christian belief works in

coaching and in leading the team. I'm never able to explain it because I don't think I can separate it. Your Christian belief permeates your whole life. Once Christ comes into your life, you're a changed person. It's not like it used to be before I accepted Christ, when I would go to church on Sunday and on Monday be back like everybody else again. Now I must express my Christian belief, whether I'm coaching football or doing something else.

The greatest witness a Christian has is living what he believes. I think that when we start talking we're unable to express what being a Christian is. Actually, I can't really explain what it means to be a Christian. I think you can only live it.

I first committed myself to Christ in 1958. Up to that time I guess I thought I was a Christian, just like a lot of other people who go to church and feel that they're good because they think they do what is right. I didn't realize at that time that I was not a Christian yet. Of course, once you make the decision to give your whole life to Christ, it makes all the difference in the world. I think that one thing a man must have to be successful and happy is peace. Christ says He gives us peace. He said, ". . . Peace I give unto you . . ." (John 14:27). I think that when you make a commitment to Christ, when you live for Him and make Him the major focal point in everything you do, your whole life revolves around Him. Then you discover the abundance He promised when He spoke about having life and having it more abundantly. This is the peace I find. There's no situation I can't cope with, because I know that He's with me all the time, and I think this is essential to a happy life.

Christianity helps you in every area of living. In coaching, everything we do is brought to public attention, and the result is that we sometimes live a very critical life, especially when things aren't going well. But I know that God has a plan for me. I don't know what it is, and I'm not really concerned about it, but just knowing it strengthens me. If it didn't, if I didn't have the faith I have, then my players would know it. They would know that I wasn't confident in myself and in where I was going, and it would start showing on them. I think, hopefully, that when they look at me in any situation they see a confident individual. They see somebody who knows where he's going and believes he's going to get there. I don't think a person can do this under the circumstances we often face unless God is directing his life.

A leader must be respected. If a person is respected sufficiently, he might even be a second stringer and still be a leader of a group or a team. When we see someone who may not be the top man in an organization or the top person on a football team, for example, and he's still a leader, it means that he probably lacks some talent to achieve the top position, but possesses all the other qualities that make a leader. In a case like that the people who are surrounding him or observing him may recognize his limitation in talent, but also recognize that he's the type of person that you can follow.

I don't believe a leader can ever be defeated in his own mind. The great men of history bear this out. Think of General MacArthur with his famous words, "I shall return"; Abe Lincoln, who was defeated over and over for office, and who finally reached the position of president; President Nixon, who was wiped out in his bid for the presidency, yet came back to obtain it. I am convinced that this is a quality every leader must have. He cannot ever afford to show doubt or he will lose his followers. Fear is present in all people, but a leader can't ever allow it to reach a point where his followers question his ability to obtain whatever he's out to obtain.

I think we feel more human in defeat than at any other time. This is when we feel our inadequacies, mostly because we are human and are unable, sometimes, to cope with our feelings and our despair. At this point I think a man who believes in God has the faith to turn around his feelings about defeat. He receives the power he needs and it strengthens him and gives him hope. I believe you have to have faith, you have to have hope to be successful, because everybody is going to suffer defeat somewhere along the line. I don't care what business you're in—if you're a teacher, a lawyer, a football coach, or a football player—you're going to be defeated sometimes and you have to have something to gain strength from so you can recover. This is what I'm able to do. It's been with me ever since I became a Christian and I've been able to overcome many suffering situations. We've had a lot of them, but each time I'm able to regroup and come back and of course this is a wonderful thing for me.

To be a leader, you must be able to accept criticism. I'm criticized quite often and it's not something that's easy to handle. I don't think many human beings can take criticism and forget it. I think there's something wrong with them if that happens. Criticism does something to you. If somebody tells you you're not confident or you're not doing right or you're not doing this or that, it hurts you. I think it makes you less effective. I know it does that to the players. It hurts players to be overcriticized, but they do need some criticism. When people are critical of me I don't close my mind to it. I'll listen to what they have to say. Are they right or are they wrong? I try to evaluate it. Do they have a point or not? I make this decision and if I think they do, then I might change a little. If I don't agree with them, I don't do anything about it.

Actually, I think any human being, when he is criticized, will tend to have a rather negative outlook. This is very human. I'm able to cope with it because I'm a natural optimist. I believe in myself. I believe in my ability as a coach. I believe in my players and their ability to come back. This gives me the strength that's necessary. It's a terrible feeling to spend a lonely night after defeat in a game. You can't sleep and of course you just don't know where you're going. It's a pretty sorry plight when you come right down to it. The only thing that can get me back is my ability to communicate with God. Then I feel new strength and purpose in myself. I'm able to regain my aims and goals after an experience like this and when it happens to me I gain a new outlook. I can overcome the negative effects of the criticism I'm expected to be subjected to in my position. I even find that at these times—and I've had many of them—there is an opportunity to be strengthened by defeat. I guess Paul said it best when he said that defeat brings on endurance and endurance brings on character and character brings on hope in God. This is the real key to success in life.

Our quarterback manual has a lot to say about leadership. The book was developed primarily by Jim Meyers, but there are a lot of things in it that we all agree on. Here are some samples: A leader is a man who exemplifies attitudes that will cause other men to follow him and produce a champion organization. There's no precise formula for leadership, but a good quarterback will not be lacking in confidence, poise, enthusiasm, alertness, courage, aggressiveness, self-control and an unquenchable desire to win.

It has often been said that one candle cannot light another without being a flame itself. By his actions, the quarterback must be most demanding of himself and show a strong desire for high expectations from his teammates. He must think of results rather than personalities. He is not trying to win a personality contest. It is the natural tendency for anyone to try to be liked by his friends and associates, but to be respected should be the leader's goal and he will find it much more gratifying than mere popularity. The greatest tribute your teammates and coaches can give you is to say, "He's a leader and a winner."

One of the most trying experiences an individual can go through is the period of doubt and soul-searching to determine whether to fight the battle or fly from it. In such a period almost unbearable tensions build up—tensions that can be relieved only by taking action one way or the other. Significantly, it is this period of crisis conduct that separates the leader from the followers. The leader is the one who has the emotional, mental and physical strength to withstand the pressures and tensions created by necessary doubts and then at the crucial moment to make a decision and act unhesitatingly. The men who fail are those who are overcome by doubts so that they either crack under the strain or flee to avoid meeting the problem at all.

On the other hand, if one is to act and lead responsibly, he must go through this period of soul-searching and testing alternate courses of action. Otherwise, he shoots from the hip, misses the target and loses the battle through sheer recklessness. As Rudyard Kipling pointed out years ago, one test of leadership is whether one has the ability to keep his head while others are losing theirs. The true leader is always ready and able to take charge and keep control.

These are some of the points we have put in our play-book for our quarterback. Respect, high expectations, enthusiasm, desire to win, courage, aggressiveness and ability to act effectively in a crisis—a leader must have them all.

I believe that a person can develop leadership at any stage of his life. As a first step, if you want to be a leader, you have to start trying to lead; you must take every opportunity you can to lead people. Do the things that you see being done by people who have the leadership qualities we're talking about. And be sure that you're a doer and not just a talker: do all the things everyone else is doing and do them better, if possible, or at least work harder at them than they do.

Another thing you've got to be sure of is your ability to organize and delegate. In a leader's role, you must impose your will on others and get them to do things. You're really organizing and directing their talents as well as your own. To do this, you must demonstrate your ability to organize yourself, because unless they respect your ability to be effective in the work you're doing—to organize your own time and get results—there's no way any follower would expect to follow you.

Some of the tools the aspiring leader should be able to work with are priority systems (systems that have been so well tested their success is practically assured), objective setting and communication so that he can inform his people exactly what the task is and what the end result should be.

Another quality that must be developed in order to achieve leadership is the ability to make a decision. This may well be the most important trait that a leader has. He must be able to gather all of the facts, evaluate them and then close his ears to everyone else and decide what should be done.

Through the years, I've made some very tough decisions and in most cases they had to do with quarterbacks. The decision to go with Don Meredith over Craig Morton and Jerry Rohms back in 1964 or '65, was crucial. When I had gathered all the facts from my experience they told me to go with Meredith, when almost everybody—including the fans, the sports writers and probably even my staff and the Cowboy organization—thought we ought to go the other way. Sometimes the facts look different to different people but your job as a leader is to gather all you know from all your associates and all your experience and make a decision. And once you make it, then go with it. One quality that prevents many people from ever becoming leaders is that they just can't make a decision and act on it.

There are not too many people who have a chance in life to reach their own particular Super Bowl—the top in their profession, whatever it may be. But I think that whether we're lawyers or doctors or young kids playing football on the junior high or senior high team, the thing that we have if we're Christians is hope. God gives us hope, He gives us direction, and even though you may have set-backs I know that with God's help you can come back, the same as I have come back. I just feel that this is what it means to be a Christian, because God doesn't make us all Super Bowl participants. He puts us into different phases of life. Wherever we are, He gives us hope in the situation we're in. And there's always a bright tomorrow because if you believe in God and have faith in Him, He guides your life. This is really what it's all about. I think God has a purpose for me and, regardless of what happens, as long as I have faith in Him I know I'm on the right track.

Carroll Dale

CARROLL DALE   Wide Receiver   Green Bay Packers

6 feet, 2 inches   200 pounds   Age—34

Virginia Polytechnic Institute

Carroll, now in his thirteenth year in pro ball, was named to *Look's* all-American team in 1959. The NEA also voted him Player-of-the-Year in the Southern Conference that year. In 1968 he was the leading scorer for the Packers. In 1969, 1970 and 1971 he was the leading receiver for the Packers and was named to Pro Bowl teams during those years. In 1969 in one game against St. Louis, he caught nine passes for 195 yards and two touchdowns. In 1970 he scored the winning touchdown in the Pro Bowl game.

Carroll is an avid outdoorsman and hunter. He and his wife, Pat, have three children. They live in Bristol, Tennessee, during the off season.

CARROLL DALE
GREEN BAY PACKERS—WIDE RECEIVER

When I was preaching at Teen Crusade in Johnson City, Tennessee, I went to a home for a snack following the meeting. There I had the chance to meet Carroll Dale and his lovely wife.

In talking about football, Carroll said to me,

It is not WINNING that is giving me the problems of life,

it is NOT winning.

I thought about that statement. When we decided to put this book together, I called Carroll and said, "Would you expand that thought into a chapter that will convey to those of us

who have the same problem

an answer to that problem?

In this chapter he tells us why!

3

WINNING

CARROLL DALE

Winning has been a part of me for as long as I can remember. Even in games around home, if I played croquet with my sister and she beat me, my reaction would be to strike out at her or to get mad and cry.

In high school, I was lucky; I didn't have to endure too much losing. But one time in basketball a team that was really marked low in the standings beat us. That night I walked the floor almost all night long.

Looking back at my life, I know I really have not always reacted in a Christlike manner. My mother set a wonderful example for me. She has lived a Christian life under stress. In other words, she had problems. For one thing, money was scarce, and I know she worked many times just to put clothes on my sister's and my back. She could have complained about having to walk a mile and a half to church, but I never heard her say anything about it. My mother always lived what she said, and even today her first concern for me is not that I win football games, but that I be a champion Christian.

I think that in my life the big problem has not been

with winning, but with not winning. I describe winning as doing the best we can at whatever we're involved in, and I often tell young people they should be obsessed with winning. Coach Vince Lombardi, whom I had the good fortune of playing under for three years at Green Bay, used to say that it took a greater team to remain a champion than it did to become a champion, and that's simply because once you're on top everyone's after you.

I think the first thing to consider about winning is how we react to a winning experience, as well as to a losing experience. Now on the winning side we see people who get too big for everybody around them. For instance, there's often a situation where a wife has worked hard to put her husband through college, and after he becomes a success that wife is no longer good enough for him. On the other hand, I've seen situations where someone has experienced failure and then blamed his wife or someone else because he lost. Of course, that's the easiest thing to do—blame someone else for our failures.

My first real losing experience came in my second year with the Los Angeles Rams, in 1961. They had traded Del Shofner, who had been All-Pro for two years, to the New York Giants and kept me, and of course I was flattered. But I had a failure that really took me back. It happened when I dropped a pass that hit me right in the numbers and fell to the ground, and I felt like all seventy-five thousand people in the Los Angeles Coliseum were putting me down. I worried so much about this that it got to a point where I couldn't even catch a ball in practice. What had happened was that I was so worried about myself that I ended up hurting both myself and the team.

So here I think I should stress the importance of not worrying about failure, because if we fear something, we will tend to cause it to come to pass. I know that this definitely happened to me in 1961 with that one little dropped pass. It turned into about fifteen or twenty dropped passes and maybe five or six lost touchdowns over a period of about six ball games, and the situation finally got to a point where I was scared to go to the huddle, or in the huddle I would be hoping that the quarterback wouldn't call a pass pattern to me.

That was a miserable way to play the game of football, and after things got that bad I felt almost like the end of the world had come. I had to sit down and have a talk with myself and see if I could get things back into perspective, which I did. I realized that I was really being very selfish. That one failure experience caused me to have more failures, which of course I really didn't want. But I caused them to come about because I was so tied up and tense.

A long time before, I had committed my life to Christ and taken the thirty-third verse of the sixth chapter of Matthew and written it in the front of my little high school scrapbook. "But seek ye first the kingdom of God, and his righteousness; and all these things shall be added unto you." This verse was a reminder that I wanted the things of God and Christ to be first, then the other good things in life would follow in their proper place.

When I thought about it from the Christian viewpoint, I saw that my experience in Los Angeles was simply a time of letting football mean too much. In the five years I was with the Rams the team did not do too well. I'm sure we didn't have a winning season. What hurt most, I think, was the fact that we had the potential to do better, and we didn't. Of course, the Los Angeles papers always tried to point out who was to blame for losing games, and the coaches did the same thing. It got to be one big merry-go-round of who's to blame, rather than people thinking constructively about trying to improve and win. Once again, I found myself caught up in this. I know that I was guilty of maybe blaming the coaches or someone else and not thinking enough about myself and how I could improve. So in '62 or '63 I really had to stop and have another talk with myself to get things back into proper perspective.

I think success is measured by how happy we are, and whether we're doing the best we can. We really have a responsibility as Christians to use the talents and abilities God has given us to their fullest potential. In other words, we shouldn't be satisfied just to kind of drift along in a so-so way and make excuses or accept mediocrity.

Now Coach Vince Lombardi was a man who stressed winning. He often quoted the famous saying that winning isn't everything, it's the only thing. And he never really admitted defeat. He was a very obsessed man as far as winning was concerned.

Sometimes I wonder why people try so hard to win. I wonder why a group of men, twenty to forty-five years old, would choose to play basketball or football, and play like it was the championships, trying to win the game. I think the reason we play games or try to be successful in business is tied right in with trying to seek first the kingdom of God and to put Christ first. I think it's a thrilling thing to compete. There's definitely nothing wrong with wanting to be the best and have high goals in life, as long as you keep the Christian perspective in sight. Then you won't use people and run over them and abuse them in trying to reach success. Instead, you'll show Christian love and consideration and empathy and concern for other people.

From a Christian standpoint, we need to be grateful to those people that helped us be successful. Actually, I don't think there's really any way we can be successful without the help of other people. I don't feel that I could be a success in the Christian life, for instance, without the help and inspiration of other Christians. And in fact, I know that we all need the fellowship of the church and of each other to grow and to keep growing and maturing as Christians.

Bart Starr is a guy who has been an inspiration to me with his winning experiences, and he achieves a lot of success. I know that his reaction to winning has not been one of cockiness, and he's always given his teammates credit. He feels that football has given a lot to him, and he's very grateful to football. Now looking at Bart, we could all say, "Well, gee, that guy has attained so much, he doesn't really have to speak to people like you or me." But Bart appreciates the value of other people. He loves the kids and tries to share with them as much as he can, with autographs and pictures and so forth.

Coach Lombardi, when he left Green Bay, told us that in spite of all the winnings and the championship and everything, championships are eventually forgotten. The money wouldn't last forever, either, he said, and the only thing that would remain—the only thing that could really last—would be spiritual. I think this is a very, very vivid statement. The fact is that there's nothing we can count on if we can lose it. I guess that's where insecurity comes from. If we want to spend our time thinking about what we can lose, we can start with the things we own and then move right on up to life itself, and that has to be an insecure feeling if that's all we have. On the other hand, if we trust in Jesus Christ we have inner peace, because we know that, no matter what, if we work and strive for Christian life we can definitely be winners.

I really can't think of anything that's greater than being a winner in Christ, because when He is our Saviour and Lord, we do have peace and joy within, and that's what I think winning is all about. That contentment, that satisfying feeling inside, and the feeling that will last is only through Christ. We can win championships, can make a lot of money, be a great success, or have a trip and escape from reality for a while, but when we come back to earth there's the same misery.

Our society is full of misery today. It is involved in serious materialistic trouble, and I think that as Christians we need to be winners in overcoming the temptation to possess things. If we think of our children and love them and discipline them and spend time with them, we can be winners in helping to build young men and women to be the citizens of tomorrow. We can try to show them through how we live that the Christian way is the only way.

I think the Bible tells us that our purpose in life is winning, that our purpose as Christians is to go out into the ends of the earth spreading the Good News of the birth, death, and Resurrection of Christ, and that we should strive to be winners for Christ. This is our mission, and I think this is where the power of the Holy Spirit comes in. It gives us the boldness to speak out, to share Christ with others, and to do it in a loving way, and not with a "holier-than-thou" attitude. Think of the woman taken in adultery who was brought to Christ. The penalty for what she had done was very serious—that of being stoned to death. But Christ simply stooped down and began to write with His finger on the ground. And when He arose He asked the woman where her accusers were. Then He told her to go and sin no more. Now here was a woman who faced the death penalty, and all of a sudden she had a chance to start over through Christ.

I look back in athletics many times, to a football season or game where I'd like to change what happened. Say after the first five games, when your record's two and three, you feel that "Gee, if we just had a chance to go back and replay those three games that we lost by a total of six or seven points, it would be great." Like my little boy when he first started playing golf: he always wanted to hit the ball over. "Daddy, can I hit that one again?" he'd ask. "Can I try it once more?" That is exactly the chance we get through Christ. We are offered a new opportunity. The Scriptures tell us that a man born again in Christ is a new man. Old things are passed away. All things have become new. So no matter what bad losers we've been or how low we are, we're offered a chance to start over, because God loves us.

In athletics there are some fundamentals that have to take place in order to be successful. First of all, you have to have desire—you have to *want* to succeed. Then you have to be willing to pay the price to do the work. You can't succeed unless you're willing to go through daily physical preparation for the game, and also mental preparation, watching and studying films, and studying plays, along with the emotional part of getting ready to cope with the game. I think, too, that *attitude* is a very big thing in success. Going back again to my problem of not catching the ball and worrying about it, what I finally did was come to a point of saying "Well, gee, this is not in continuity with my expressed goal." What I really wanted most was to put Christ first.

So I finally think I've matured. Through the years I've gotten so I can pray this prayer: "Lord, help me play to the best of my ability, for the good of the team and to Your glory, and keep me and my teammates and the members of the other team free of injury." Now I can just play the game to enjoy it, not letting it take first place, and that's what I have been striving for during the last few years. If I catch a pass, great. If I don't, though it still hurts, I try to forget it as soon as possible.

So you've got to remember the winning experiences and forget the failure experiences. Profit from the failure experiences, but don't dwell on them. It's just like playing the game of golf. If you think about missing a putt or missing the shots, chances are you're going to miss. But if you think you can do it, then you can.

I mentioned that exercise is fundamental for an athlete in preparation for the game, and the Bible bears out that we should strive to grow and bear fruit. In order to do this, we need to have daily exercises, spiritual exercises in the Christian life so that we may grow and mature and be possessed with the Word of God. So a daily quiet time or devotional period is vital along with fellowship with other Christians, reading, praying, attending church, and sharing Christ with others—especially through our example of how we live, but also, of course, by word of mouth when we have the opportunity.

Not long ago, I received a questionnaire from someone who was going to write some articles about how faith related to one's playing the football game, or to getting ready for the game emotionally. I wrote the person and told him I didn't feel the faith was worth very much if it was just used on Sunday mornings through a team devotion, or if it was a faith that someone had just for the game. I feel that Christianity is something we live each day, and that is the way it becomes a part of the football game.

Bobby Richardson was once asked if being a Christian made him a better baseball player, and after thinking a moment he said, "Well, I guess knowing Christ makes me a better father. So I guess it makes me a better baseball player, too."

Well, I also feel that it definitely does make one a better father or a better mother, daughter, or son, but this personal relationship with Christ does not guarantee success in any field. I feel that what it will do is help us to reach our potential and use the talents that we have. And if we're following Christ we have to be understanding and compassionate toward our children and our mates. Then we will have consideration in the home, and, of course, love.

As far as business and the Christian life is concerned, I feel that as Christians we'll be less distracted by sin and by greed for material things. We'll be able to be honest businessmen, or professional people, and everyone will know they can depend on us. In the long run this good reputation will result in helping business, because nowadays it is difficult to find someone in business that you can trust or even a person who will do an honest day's work. I feel that we have a Christian obligation here, an obligation to do a full day's work for a day's pay. This is the Christian thing to do, and we're not to try to get by with doing as little as we can.

Carrying this same idea over to athletics, I feel that athletes have an opportunity to use God-given talent. Now don't misunderstand: I don't mean that just because a young man might become a Christian he will be a great professional athlete. I do mean that he will be a team man, though, and that he will keep the training rules and be out there playing the game to his fullest ability—with enthusiasm, hard work, and dedication. As a result, a Christian athlete should come closer to realizing his potential and being the best athlete he can be—and of course, doing his best as far as the team is concerned.

I've often wondered how a team made up of, say, forty dedicated men, unconditionally sold out to Christ, would perform. I think that team would be out there fighting till the last whistle, doing its best. In other words, it would be a team the fans could be proud of, and could identify with. Even if the team got beaten, everyone would know that the players had put forth their greatest effort, and no one would be ashamed of them.

I have differed a little with some Christian friends of mine, who feel that if you want a world championship, that's what you go out and pray for. As I mentioned earlier, I don't pray to win, and I really don't think God cares who wins the football game. I feel that He cares about our motives, our desires, and priorities—in other words, why we're playing the game. I know that many teams in the National Football League have Christian men, but I don't feel that if a team has six Christians playing to win they'll win because they're praying. They might definitely *help* a team win, because they should be unselfish men; they should be leaders, playing for the good of the team. So six Christian men on a team—or ten, or twelve—should be a plus, but just because one team has more Christians than another doesn't mean anything about the outcome of the game.

In my own life, being a Christian has helped me enjoy football more. Through Christian maturity I've learned to play the game and enjoy it and keep everything in perspective most of the time. The only recent time I think I've let my priorities get too confused was in 1970, during exhibition season. We were undefeated, and I felt that we had a pretty good football team. Then we opened up with the Detroit Lions, and everything went wrong. Quarterback Norman Snead went for 76 yards against us, and we got beat forty to nothing.

Now, as I said earlier, all of us should hate to lose and be upset when we do lose, and I'm no exception to that. After that game my jaw was hanging low, and I was feeling very bad, in a state of shock when I went to the locker room.

On Monday we were all moping around and wondering what happened and then in my mail I received a package. When I opened it, I found a picture of a man and his kids and me together. I remembered this man from training camp of that year, when I had posed for photographs with him and his family. He enclosed a letter asking me to autograph the picture and reminding me that at the time the picture was made his wife was suffering from the same terminal illness Coach Lombardi had. Then he said that his wife had died three days after Coach Lombardi. That made me realize how much I had to be thankful for, and how I really needed a kick in the seat of the pants for being so low about getting beaten forty to nothing in a football game.

Coach Lombardi used to say that the harder you work, the harder it is to surrender, and I feel it's the same way about all of life. In athletics the harder you work and prepare, the harder it is to give up. In a Christian life the more we strive—no matter what the setbacks might be, even if we get knocked down in the game of life—we get back up more determined to go on for Christ. Sometimes it would be so easy to give up. When it's hard to win I like to remember two well-known athletic sayings. They may be trite, but they're still true: When the going gets tough, the tough do get going. And it's not the size of the dog in the fight that counts; it's the fight in the dog.

Roger Staubach

Roger Staubach   Quarterback   Dallas Cowboys

6 feet 3 inches   197 pounds   Age—30
United States Naval Academy

Roger, now in his fourth season of pro ball, must be noted as one of the outstanding college players of all time. All-American for two years, he was named by both AP and UPI as the Back-of-the-Year. He won both the Maxwell and Heisman trophies and in 1965 captained the All-Star squad in the college All-Star game in Chicago. He spent four years as an officer in the Navy, one of which was in Vietnam.

Last season he was pro football's leading passer with 59.7 percent completions. He was the first quarterback with less than five years' experience to lead his team to a championship since 1945.

After the 1971 season, he was voted the most valuable player in the NFL and the most valuable player in the Super Bowl.

Roger and his wife, Marianne, have three daughters. During the off season, he deals in commercial real estate in Dallas.

ROGER STAUBACH
DALLAS COWBOYS—QUARTERBACK

I first met Roger in his rookie year as a Cowboy, following a chapel service. I was greatly impressed with his interest in what was said for Christ and his willingness to want to share this with other young people.

This year, following one of the Cowboys' crucial games, I was riding on the team bus with Roger.

He had an injury.

"Roger," I said, "the team is going to have a great season and you are doing very well. Promise me one thing—that as a Christian, you will give God the honor and glory for all He does through you this season."

He turned to me and said, "Billy, I promise you that I will give God the honor and the glory."

When he won the Maxwell trophy this year and it was announced in the paper, I called his home.

"Roger—congratulations!"

His opening line to me was:

"Thank you, but I've already given God the honor and the glory for that trophy."

This is true about Roger Staubach. He realizes men's applause will fade very quickly.

Roger Staubach is a man who is disciplined for God. His life puts in action the things he tells people about Jesus Christ.

Following the victory in the Super Bowl of 1972, Roger's life proved that he believes in the life of the big picture beyond football.

It is not that he discounts the importance of football.

It is that he knows the importance of his life counting for Jesus Christ.

4

SUCCESS

ROGER STAUBACH

On the subject of success, the important thing is keeping your perspective. Winning or gaining fame is relative to the situation and when the situation changes you must be able to adjust. You have to realize that if you're not successful the next year, then the friends you have just accumulated won't be around anymore. However, if you haven't changed as a person, the ones you've always had will still be there.

I went through this in my junior year at the Naval Academy. I received a lot of plaudits, requests and awards and won the Heisman Trophy, but I found out that fame is fleeting. When I went into the service and was away from football for a while, I was just Roger Staubach—married, family man—and this is the way I was treated, with some exceptions, after four years away from the game.

Remembering that has helped me put things in perspective and I haven't let it go to my head. I realize who are the true friends I've always had. A lot of things are superficial. People are nice but they are fickle; unless you continue to perform, they're gone. That's why I try to size a person up, not just how he does in athletics or whatever job he has, but what he is as an overall person. The kind of individual he really is and his belief in God are extremely important to me.

I've always believed, even before this success, that I could achieve it. I've believed that for two reasons: because of my own self-confidence and also because I'm on a tremendous team with fine individuals. When you're surrounded by good people, your own self-confidence, as far as being an athlete is concerned, is very important. I just believed that what did happen could happen and I believed that very strongly. I never doubted it. But once it's been achieved you can't pat yourself on the back because right away you're on trial again. That's the way people are; they keep you on trial. As athletes, that's something we must realize.

Oh, yes, I do have a desire to relax, to be myself. They equate an athlete with the idea that the more praise he receives, the more it becomes an ego thing. But life to me isn't just the life we're in today. There's something much greater. I'm not on any kind of ego trip. In fact, one of the things I don't like about professional football is being in the limelight, being badgered, especially if you're successful like we were.

I do like the game. I like to be good to the people, I don't want to turn them off, but I would just like to be myself, as well as being a successful athlete. I like to compete—I like to win. This is something that's in my nature, but it's not going to be the end of the world if I'm hurt or if I'm unsuccessful or people don't pat me on the back anymore, because I'm not crazy about that anyway; I know most of it is superficial.

If this were the end, if everything that was inside of you

were based on now in this life, I could see trying to achieve everything you possibly could, as fast as possible. If you didn't achieve it in this life everything would be lost. I do think that we need to do our very best and achieve whatever we can within our means and within the boundaries that we have and the rules that God has given us. But to me, there's something much greater later on and all the wealth and all the praise and all the fame that we can achieve now is not that long or that lasting. If we don't achieve it, that's just the way it goes.

This gets into a philosophy that I have: I believe in God and in His overall plan for us. And while we've got to try to do the very best we can now, there are much, much greater things ahead for us.

I base my entire life and the way I treat my family on my belief in Christ as Saviour and the way that I believe He would want me to live this life. I base it on the chance to be with Him in eternity. Non-Christians may think that's a corny outlook but that doesn't bother me. I personally am willing to build my life on my Christian belief and my certainty of being with Christ someday. On our team, we have a lot of players who are basically Christian men and they have this kind of faith, also.

Of course, the top honor for a team in all of professional football is the Super Bowl. That is looked on as the most important game the team can play, so it is naturally the most important game in the Dallas Cowboy's life. But there's an even greater honor—greater than any pro football has to offer—and that is the honor of knowing Jesus Christ.

I think it is true that God has given me a talent as an athlete. I think this is the extra thing He has given me— He's given everyone something. This is an area that I've tried to develop fully. I've spent time in the service. I've got a college degree. I think I'm completely normal as far as being able to do many things. I think I could be successful as a businessman, or in some other field, but I've always gone right back into athletics. My desires, my wants, are in that area—in the competition of playing and the skill that I like to show and use.

Defeat touches me very strongly, whether I'm defeated in a bad day of practice or in shooting foul shots in basketball against someone, or even playing ping-pong. But of course in professional football, defeat of the team I'm on has a very definite, and much more powerful, effect on me. One time, we lost to Minnesota. I played in the game—I had a chance to help the team win. True, I came in late when we were already behind, but it almost gives you the feeling after it's over that you want to say, "What the heck am I doing playing the game when I feel this bad about losing?" Of course, the following day you can't wait to compete again! I think that if you're a natural competitor defeat is very hard to take. They say you learn things from losing, but I haven't learned too much from it, except that it's just a terrible feeling to lose.

I'm speaking now from the viewpoint of a back-up quarterback. When I got out of the service and joined the Cowboys, it was a big thrill to be with a team that had a great possibility of winning the championship. I was fortunate to be able to start early in the year and get a good feeling about the team and to feel a part of it. And while I would like to be behind the center every Sunday as a starter, it's an accomplishment just to be a part of this group—and of course you become a part of the team's success, too. We won five games that year. Then we went into the play-offs and won two more, so that made seven in a row. It's a great feeling to be on a team that has come back and put their guts on the field like the Cowboys did to get to the Super Bowl.

How did we do it? It's hard to say, there are so many factors. Football, I feel, is really about 50 percent mental; feelings have a lot to do with it. That doesn't discount the ability; it has to be there, too. Now, there's no question that the Cowboys have the ability, but I think emotions were so strained after our disastrous defeat by St. Louis that people were counting us out. I think our general attitude—our feelings of pride as athletes—changed quite a bit around that time. And I think it was this change in attitude that helped us win. We just started, I think, playing one game at a time. I guess pride took over and before we knew it we were the Eastern Division champions and were in the play-offs.

As for myself, again I say athletics are just relative to my ultimate goal. That goal is not throwing a thousand touchdown passes. This isn't spiritual or religious. I'm not what I want to be yet; I'm trying to improve in this area, but as I say, my situation is just relative to my ultimate goals. When the saturation point is reached will be hard to say; I'm not in the game just to see how many awards I can receive. I've been up and I've been down. It hasn't been just a straight-up track for me, because I was there, as I say, as a college athlete and then when I came back to pro football I was the kid that was stupid to come back. "Four years in the service—he won't be back." "Another Heisman Trophy flop." These were things that were said when I went down. Now I'm starting to come back again.

It didn't bother me personally when I was down. Of course, it was a matter of pride, but as far as affecting my life and the things that are important to me, it didn't.

There was a desire to try to get back—not for praise or fame or awards, but because this is the area in which I want to be successful. I believed I could get back and I did. And of course, with an athlete—just as with an entire team—when you have the chance to come back and you do it, it's a fantastic feeling. But reaching the saturation point could happen very easily and I could get hurt next year and never play again, and still my life would be here for something much greater, not just for now.

Being known can have its advantages as far as your effect on others. That would be about the only reason it could really matter to me how I'm described. I've done a lot of appearances—speaking engagements and this and that. Some of it has been business and I was paid for that. But on other occasions I've done it because it gave me a platform to tell other people what I think is really important in life.

I want what is said about me to be true and I like it to be said if it can have a good effect on someone else's life, but when it comes to the kind of person I really am, I'd have a hard time telling anyone how to describe me. Some people overexaggerate me completely and some underestimate me. I just like to be known for what I honestly am and as far as what is written or said about me, I really couldn't care less about trying to establish the image or to be somebody. I want to be somebody in the eyes of God, not in the eyes of So-and-So. This is what is important to me.

It was often talked about in the Super Bowl—what my feeling was. Was I praying to win? Would I be disappointed if we lost? But those questions are really irrelevant. The fact is that I asked God to just let me do the very best I could. I've heard too many people say that

when they turned to God they then went on to win. I don't
think it works that way. I don't understand His will or
why He does things and that's why faith is critical in my
life.

Whether or not we won the Super Bowl, my attitude
toward God would not have changed at all. He is going
to give us what He wants to give us and that is why I
didn't pray to win, but only that I would do my best. I was
hoping for the best but if we had lost I would not have
been disappointed.

I've had faith through thick and thin in my life. When
I'm winning I thank God. And when I've come to a point
where there has been a problem or tragedy, I've stayed
with Him then, also. What's important is to have faith in
His will, and not just pray to win and be successful, because there's so much more in life than just our success
here.

Jim Houston

JIM HOUSTON   Linebacker   Cleveland Browns

6 feet 3 inches   236 pounds   Age—34
Ohio State University

Jim, now in his thirteenth year in pro ball, is a quiet, dedicated leader both on and off the field. He was acquired by the Browns in the first round draft in 1960 and since that time has been "Mr. Dependable." In 1962, he was called to active duty as a lieutenant in the United States Army. For the past nine seasons, he has been a regular linebacker and was named to the Pro Bowl for four seasons.

Jim, his wife, Barbara, and their five children live in Ghent, Ohio, near Akron, where he is a successful regional manager of a life insurance company and a developer of residential real estate sub-divisions.

JIM HOUSTON
CLEVELAND BROWNS—LINEBACKER

Jim Houston was faithful to the chapel services of the Cleveland Browns. Following one of these services,
    after a great message and some personal time with Bill Glass, Jim Houston became a Christian.
I remember talking to him before he knew Christ. He was very interested, but as Jim himself says,

> My interest was not enough.
> Even a good life was not enough.
> I had to let Christ be my Saviour.

Because of his consistent play,
    because of his knowledge on the field,
        his teammates elected him Defensive Captain.
Because of these same attributes,
    I have asked him to write on living for Christ.

5

LIVING FOR CHRIST

JIM HOUSTON

I am thankful to God for the opportunity to share my testimony with various groups so that they might understand and accept Christ. I remember sharing with some of our teammates the really great experience I had in relating Christ to a friend and seeing him come to the knowledge of Christ as Saviour. It always amazes me that God would use me to tell others who He is.

I guess that when you talk about Jim Houston and his Christian experience you talk about a guy who, I feel, always lived a straight and true life. I had a good mother to guide and direct me, and a good father—a great family living experience, with five brothers and a sister, all older than I am.

Now when you talk to a guy who's a committed Christian, from that kind of background, you expect to hear of some dynamic happening that brought about a radical change in his life. Really, though, when I look back at the early days and the early experiences I had when I went to church, there just doesn't seem to have been much that happened. My mom went to church sometimes. Dad never went that I can recall. We just weren't religiously oriented, but we felt that we were good people—honest and trust-worthy. I think that we probably were in a category with most of the other Americans in this country: church didn't mean that much to us, so we didn't go regularly. I did have a brother who was a committed Christian and I went to his church sometimes, but I really didn't get much out of it. As a result I just wasn't in tune with a true Christian experience.

In the mid-sixties, Bill Glass was instrumental in trying to get Jesus Christ's word to professional football players. He went to Blanton Collier and asked if he could conduct chapel services for the team. I agreed that we should try it and used a little influence and Blanton went along with us. At the first service the rookies and a few of the veterans showed up and that was the beginning of a fine chapel service program. Over the years we have been able to get many excellent speakers. These men have been directly responsible, not only for my committing myself to Jesus Christ in a very definite Christian way, but for many other individuals taking the same step.

My first meaningful Christian experience was down in New Orleans in about 1968. We had just listened to Bob Harrington, at his fiery, dynamic best, and while I really wasn't at a loss, all I could think of at the time was, "Well, there *is* somewhat of an empty feeling." I wasn't exactly groping in the dark, but I did want to know more about this eternal life. What was it all about?

On Saturday night, after our meeting with Bob Harrington and prior to our New Orleans game on Sunday, I asked Bill to explain. He took me to his room and began by telling me, "Jim, there is nothing complicated about accepting Jesus Christ as your Saviour. Just confess your sins to

Him and ask Him to receive you. That's all you have to do. There's nothing magic about it. Then you have to pray and to grow by reading the Bible and by listening to others who can help you grow in the spirit." You know, nothing really exciting happened to me at that particular time and I don't know whether anything exciting has happened since, but suddenly there just seemed to be an answer. It's so simple I wish everyone could realize that all you have to do to have Jesus come into your life is to say, "Here I am" and ask Him to take over. I think the biggest problems come when we try to follow His teachings, because, after all, we are human and weak. In my own case, it has helped to talk to Jesus through prayer and He's helped me a tremendous amount in allowing me to become a more mature person and to have a deeper understanding of what life is all about.

I think that in trying to follow Jesus' teachings we find strength to cope with the daily trivialities that can foul up our thinking and create arguments. My wife, who is also a committed Christian, has indicated to me that she noticed a change in our life together from about 1968 or '69, which was just after the time I had talked to Bill. My total objective now is to try to live as Jesus would want me to live and as long as I can do that I know I'm accomplishing something.

I have certain goals to strive for and I hope I can achieve those goals during my life. For one thing, I want my five children to grow up as Christians. My son just took his catechism and he understands what most of it is all about now. I want all five of my kids to be strong in their good influence on others.

Right now my main feeling is that I'm not studying the Bible enough. And frankly, I don't think I work hard enough at trying to get converts. I'm involved with the Billy Graham Crusade, for instance, and I really haven't done that much; I haven't worked that hard at it. While it's true that I won't be around when the Crusade is on, I feel that I should have done more, anyway. Then, too, I'm involved in a real estate development and I just haven't taken out enough time from that for work on the Crusade. I think that one of the most important problems Christians have to face up to is that we don't take enough time to bring the word of Jesus to everyone else.

I had a chance to put in a word or two recently in the adult Sunday school class at the Zion United Methodist Church in Montrose, Illinois, a community to which I just moved. The class is kind of open and I suggested that during the summer we have each member take over and discuss whatever he or she wanted. I was picked to teach the first two hours and my topic was, "What is the greatest single thing in the world?" There were about twenty-five in the class—attorneys, engineers, accountants and so on— and their general summation was that love, or love in Jesus Christ's light, is the greatest thing in the world.

I learned a lot from teaching that class, basing the lesson on 1 Corinthians, chapter 13. Almost everyone in the group professed this great love. Then I asked them what they would think of a black person moving in next door. Right away they started qualifying everything by saying that it wouldn't matter what the color of his skin was as long as he was a good person. Generally I think that sounds like a good solution, but Jesus wants us to go a little bit further than that—He wants us to accept him and help him *even if he's not all that good a person.* My objective in teaching the lesson was to bring it across to the class that Jesus would accept whomever it was that moved next door, regardless of whether he had been a murderer, a rapist, or what. I think that Jesus' teachings clearly tell us that we should accept everyone.

I don't know for sure whether I would put conditions on who my neighbor might be, but most of the class members did: these individuals are all fairly well-to-do; they are educated people who understand generally what Jesus' teachings are. But in spite of that they came right back and put conditions on their acceptance of their fellow man. I was concerned, because I wanted to get the point across that our objective as fallible human beings is to grow to know Jesus and understand Him and His teachings—and even more importantly, not to make up our own minds but to follow what He says and try to guide others in His way. I just hope I made this clear and that I was able to influence even one person's thinking a little bit that day.

I have another hang-up—well, it's not really a hang-up, but I have difficulty in getting across to my brothers and to my children just how important this relationship to Jesus is. I'm concerned about this, and I hope that some day, some way, every one of them will receive Jesus Christ as I have, as personal Saviour and guide. Your whole life seems to change once you accept Jesus into it. It's a great feeling and I want everyone in my family to share it. My concern doesn't stop with my own family, of course. I hope that, not only during the rest of my football career, but also during the rest of my life, I'll be able to influence others for Christ and bring them to an understanding of why I'm committed to Him and His teachings.

Bob Vogel

BOB VOGEL   Offensive Tackle   Baltimore Colts

6 feet 5 inches   260 pounds   Age—30
Ohio State University

Now in his tenth year in pro ball, Bob had a great career
at Ohio State. A three-year regular, he was team captain
in his senior year, was United Press All-American, played
in the East-West and Hula Bowls. He has played in the
Pro Bowl four times during his pro career. Colts' head
coach Don McCafferty said of him, "He is a dedicated,
methodical technician who takes great pride in his work."

Bob and his wife, Andrea, have two daughters. They live
on a farm in Havre de Grace, Maryland. He is a partner in
one of the largest hog raising enterprises in the country
and is an executive with an employment agency in Baltimore.

BOB VOGEL
BALTIMORE COLTS—OFFENSIVE TACKLE

Bob Vogel has faith in Jesus Christ—
    and that faith has been tested.
    A test of faith can make a man strong or weak in his
faith. Because of the experiences Bob has had and the tests
that he has gone through both on and off the football field,
I asked him to write this chapter.
    I trust you may be able

> to share with him—
> to share his emotional tests,
> to share his hardships,
> to share his anxieties,

    so that you can develop your own faith—
    a faith that will create strength in you during your time

> of adversity
> of insecurity
> of doubt.

Bob Vogel can say,
    "Lord, I believe: help thou mine unbelief."

I am sure *his* belief will help *yours!*

6

FAITH

BOB VOGEL

The Christian faith is a positive force—not a negative one. It is a source of strength. It offers us challenge and excitement. However, this is nullified very frequently in the current mood in our society and our church. When I go to church, I'm unfavorably impressed with a lot of the songs we sing. My concept of Christian joy is to be able to sing a song and smile and feel your heart full. But so many of the songs we sing are almost like funeral dirges. They're extremely difficult, extremely solemn. To their credit, the black churches in our country have really caught the mood of Christianity. They feature a little handclapping, a hallelujah or two, a little shouting, a lot of enthusiasm. I find that extremely attractive and I wish that in the white churches we could be a little less staid and a little less whatever we are and get down to the point of having some real joy in our singing.

I also dislike the solemnity of the service in many churches. It's almost as if we're approaching a God that we can't even touch or reach and it looks as if some people are afraid to raise their eyes up to the altar for fear of being

blinded or something. There's a reverence—almost a fear—
that I don't think ought to exist there. I don't mean to
minimize the fact that when we're in God's house we ought
to have a sense of reverence, but at the same time knowing
how much He loves us, we ought to be able to go there and
smile and have real joy, too.

This attitude of lacking joy, of being defeated, is a
problem that perhaps our whole country is going through
today. I think it was reflected very well in Ezekiel 37,
verses one through fourteen. Evidently this was written at
the time when the Jews had been dispersed. They were in
a very difficult situation. It appeared that all of their lives
were crumbling in front of them. They had no chance to
realize their dreams of being a nation—being united and
having something solid—and at this point in their time, the
people thought there was absolutely no future for them.
Then God provided Ezekiel with a vision of a valley of
dead bones and in the vision God asked him if he thought
those bones would be able to come to life. Ezekiel answered, "Well, Lord, you know what the situation is."
Then God asked him to tell the bones that they could be
alive and come back together again. Ezekiel did exactly
as God had suggested, and lo and behold, the bones did
get together. They were dried out and bleached by the
sun, but God had promised that He would give them
sinews and flesh, and that He would put them back together. When He had done that, the only thing that re-
mained was for God to breathe life into them, which He
did. Perhaps we can equate God's breathing life into
those dull and lifeless bones with what can happen to us
if we allow the power of the Holy Spirit to work in our
lives.

I believe that negativism is one of the real problems we

face today. Some churches I've been in almost seem to follow the old-time orthodox Jewish faith, with hundreds of rules to abide by. Very frequently, you hear the parents or the elder statesmen in the church saying to the young people, "Don't dance, don't smoke, don't drink, don't go to the movies, don't do this and don't do that, or you're going to go to hell. Your life-style is damned." Now admittedly some of those are not always the best things to do, but instead of stressing the "don'ts" you've got to offer something positive.

Let's say a salesman walks into your office selling a copying machine. Suppose he were to say, "This machine will last you for twenty years and it will cost you eight cents a copy." Then he packs up his bag and leaves. You would be sitting there saying, "How does this relate to me? What are the benefits involved?" Then suppose that right behind him comes another salesman, who says, "Our machine will last for twenty years, too. Besides, we have a big advantage; each copy will cost you only six cents. And we have a direct distributorship whereby we can supply your paper at a rate that no one else can match. Now, another thing is that we have a very attractive service warranty . . ." and he goes on giving you reasons why you ought to buy his machine.

Now if we are so involved with the negative aspects of our faith, we're not really giving people a reason to try it out; all we're doing is telling them that once they get involved, they have this immense bunch of rules and regulations to live by. How does this strike a young person, say someone fifteen or sixteen years of age? You approach this young fellow or gal about the Christian faith and you say, "I think you ought to have a right relationship with God." They ask why, and you say, "Well, so that when you die, you can have salvation and be with God in heaven." Now the young people are very critical today and they want to know all the reasons, so this young person says to himself, "All right. That sounds very attractive. At the end of my life I can have this right relationship with God, and I can live with Him in heaven. But you see, I'm fifteen, and life expectancy for me is somewhere in the seventies, so I'm sitting here with more than fifty years to live. Now, what is this guy God going to do for me during the next fifty years?" If we can't convey to people what the relevancy of a Christian life is now—today, while they're alive—we're going to be like the first copying salesman. We may have something attractive, but unless we can tell people about the day-to-day values of the Christian faith, we're not likely to make very many sales.

What I'd like to talk about here is the relevancy of our Christian faith and the power we can receive from it. During the course of our team Bible study, we have been discussing the New Testament. A very important reference source for us is the series that William Barclay has written on the various New Testament books. Barclay is obviously very impressed with a word that he uses a number of times. It's a Greek word and the translation is roughly that, once having been through a difficult situation, a person is better off for having gone through it. Also, it refers to the power to go through such situations, to be able to challenge them and say, "Ok, I'm in a bind, but there is a power that can give me strength and allow me to win out."

One of the examples that Barclay gives relates to a young man in his mid-twenties, the poet William Ernest Henley. He was healthy, virile and strong, but his legs had been severely damaged in an accident. Then infection set in and the doctors decided that the only thing they could do would be to amputate a foot. Now, by all rights, this young man would have to face up to the fact that his life was finished, especially since they didn't have the artificial limbs then that they have now. But he was later able to write the poem *Invictus,* which begins, "Out of the night that covers me, black as the pit from pole to pole, I thank whatever gods may be for my unconquerable soul." To me, that's exciting, because here was a guy whose life was potentially wiped out, but who could give thanks for a powerful attitude, for the possibility of going forward from that particular point.

In the New Testament, one of the most exciting characters is a guy named Peter and I think we can see the relevancy and power of our faith from taking a look at his life. At the Last Supper, when Christ had said, "You know, one of you guys is going to deny me," Peter really took exception to this. "Well, Lord, it won't be me," he said, "because you and I are tight." And yet, after Christ was captured, Peter was confronted three times by people who asked whether he was part of that radical group that had caused so much trouble and three times Peter denied a knowledge of Christ.

Now, after the Holy Spirit had been sent to give the disciples the support they needed, there was a dramatic change in Peter and there is apparently only one explanation: the power that God had given him. Contrast the Peter who could not face a woman and say, "Yes, I was with Jesus" with the Peter who offered his life as a sacrifice so that he could tell people about Christ. When Peter would come into a town it caused a great deal of concern, because, wherever he went, the town fathers and the soldiers were very much against him. The Roman authori-

ties were afraid that Christianity could overrun their area
and overthrow their power. And of course the Jews, the
Pharisees and the Sadducees were concerned that the new
religion Peter talked about would take away *their* power.
So, for various reasons, almost everybody was interested in
squashing the new faith. Peter would come into a town,
and the guys would say, "Peter, you can't do your thing
here. If you do, we're going to put you in jail; we're going
to beat you." But the new Peter never let this detract from
what he was doing. He just kept going out and talking
about his faith and he was always available to serve. Now,
here was a guy who put his life on the line, a guy who was
in jail much of the time, but yet one who previously
couldn't confess to a woman that he knew Jesus. I think
that is a perfect example of the power that is available
to us.

Another guy in the New Testament who really impresses
me is Paul, not only because of the wisdom his writing
makes available to us today, but also because of the very
dynamic change he underwent within his personality and
his life-style. At the beginning, Paul was foremost in the
ranks of the anti-Christians. In fact, he was in charge of
making sure that Christianity didn't grow, of ferreting out
the Christian troublemakers. Then one day on the road,
Paul was confronted by the power of God. He was blinded
and went through a very dramatic faith change. What
shows here the relevancy in the power of the Christian faith
is that all of a sudden Paul had to account to his former
friends and colleagues for this change within his life. Now
we as new Christians are faced with this same situation.
We cannot become Christians and not have our lives
change dramatically. So how do we deal with the people
we used to associate with? They are bound to notice that

there have been some changes. Paul handled it head-on. He had the ability to say, "Look, man, I've had this exceptional experience and now I'm a different person. I have a different sense of values and my priorities have changed."

One of the things that frequently defeats a new Christian is that when he is away on a retreat, or has had a very significant experience at church, or has been one-to-one with his pastor and has decided to make a commitment, he feels just great, because he's in a sheltered situation. But then he leaves the shelter. He goes out into the world of his friends and associates and all of a sudden he has to be able to say, "This thing has happened to me!" That is when he hears his friends asking, "What are you—some kind of a Holy Roller or Jesus Freak?" All of a sudden his confidence starts to erode. The great feeling he had about Jesus is washed away and frequently he succumbs to the peer-group pressure. The thing that impressed me about Paul is that there was the Jew of all Jews, born into the hierarchy, having achieved a great office within the upper realm of the whole Jewish world and suddenly he became a new person. I know there had to be times when Paul felt very funny about having his friends challenge him, but yet, in the face of all this, he stood strong. That is what's exciting.

When we stop to take a look at the people close to us, one of the frightening things is that whether they are young or old, many of them often look the same, talk the same, act the same and have the same sense of values, simply because they don't have the courage to form their own value patterns. They refuse to take a particular stand if their friends won't back them up. I like the fact that I know God loves me and is going to support me. If my peer group is involved with something and I don't agree with them, I can feel confident that, if I'm in the right, God will supply the strength I need.

I like being different. I like having a power. The thing that's exciting to me is that by being a Christian and relying on God's power, you can be your own man. Another thing to consider is this: If what you want to be involved in is right and your friends are putting you down, are they really friends?

Concerning my own personal existence in talking about the relevancy and the power of a Christian existence, when I came into the National Football League I had graduated from Ohio State University and I had had a good high school and college career. Because of my superior size and ability, along with some other qualities, I had not often faced anyone who represented a serious challenge. In college I was a good size at 238 pounds, while at that weight I was a midget for the NFL. I found myself confronted by men who weighed from 270 to 300 pounds and who had extreme ability and strength.

We went into the exhibition season and I was playing against Doug Atkins of the Chicago Bears. He defeated me soundly. Everything I tried to do he just destroyed and for the very first time I began to wonder whether or not I could compete as a pro. When we went into the first game of the regular season we played against the New York Giants and I was confronted by Andy Robustelli, a guy who's now in the NFL Hall of Fame. I did nothing that day to keep him out of the Hall of Fame. In fact, I think I contributed a great deal that year to a lot of guys getting a lot of votes for all sorts of all-star teams. The pressure was really extreme because I was a baby on the offensive line. The next youngest guy was Jim Parker, who had been nine times all-pro.

At this time, I remembered the Bible stories about the power and the peace God can give in time of need. So I began praying. I said, "All right, Lord. My life is really strung out. For the first time, I'm questioning whether I can really compete and whether or not I can cope in this new environment." And I began praying that God would help me deal with the problem. Now it wasn't that I became an effective offensive tackle all of a sudden, in just a flash of light. Rather, it was just that God gave me the ability to deal with the mistakes I made and to keep from letting them destroy me. Bit by bit, I began to develop confidence in what I was doing. All through my career with the Colts there have been the exciting championships, but along with them came the horrendous defeats that just cut your heart out of you and broke your soul and your mind and your body. But all during this time, even through the most difficult periods we've had, there has been one place I've always been able to go. When I'm tired, when I'm not playing well, I can go to God and simply ask Him for support. It's not as if He reaches down and blocks the guy for me, or reaches down and pumps the extra energy into me. It's just a source of strength that I can go to and very frequently the fact that God cares for me is all I need to know in order to deal with whatever the problem is. There are many times when my legs are very, very tired and they feel almost made of wood, when my heart feels like it's going to pound out of my chest with fatigue, and it has really been surprising to me that when I just pray, "Lord, I need Your help to support me now," that power is there and it's available.

Within my own family, there have been instances when I have felt the relevance and power of God's love. Before our first daughter was born, my wife and I prayed that, first of all, God would allow us to have a family and secondly, that our children would be healthy. However, we also prayed that, if the second prayer couldn't be answered, God would give us the ability to deal with whatever problems there might be. The reason we were able to do some advance planning on this is that my wife is a registered nurse and she has spent a good deal of time in the obstetrics section of the hospital. She saw the newborn children and frequently she saw one born with some sort of problem. Knowing this was a possibility, we decided to pray about it in advance.

We had been praying this way for about two years and when our baby was born she had a very serious birth defect. My first reaction was to lash out at God. "You know, you're really some kind of a God," I said. "I've spent two years praying, and if this is the way you answer prayer, you have a funny way of dealing with people's desires." One thing that hurt was that there are so many children born in the towns around us who are strictly the product of passion and no one really cares whether they live or die and all we wanted was just one healthy child to love and share life with. I was angry and I was hurt and confused and afraid and everything else, but we still had to make a decision as to what we were going to do about her. The doctor had explained that the particular surgery required was risky. We faced three possibilities: the child might die; or if she survived she could be a vegetable, with seriously decreased mental powers; or she could survive the surgery in good shape. Well, when you've got three chances and two of them aren't good, it really puts you into a bind. I'm not sure how it happened, but my wife and I did a very significant thing: We simply took our baby and said, "God, we want to put Heidi into Your hands; we want to ask that Your will be done and not ours and we'll just trust in the fact that You love us and You're going to do the thing that's best."

We knew what the surgical procedure was. It involved major skull surgery, exposing the brain and all the problems that can result from that, especially when the baby weighs only a little more than seven pounds and is just a bit over a week old. Once we had committed her into God's hands, we just sat in the waiting room with the strangest sense of calm and peace. I could sit there and read a magazine and say to myself, "You know, you're not afraid." And I knew that the reason I wasn't afraid was that I had asked God for help and I believed that He wanted to help us, that He loved us and that whatever happened, He'd be there for us to trust in. When you can get that kind of support from your God, you know that He is both real and relevant.

In the summer of 1971, doctors found what appeared to be cancerous material in my dad's left lung. During exploratory surgery they discovered that the cancer had spread to such an extent that it was inoperable. This hit me like a bolt of lightning, because it told me that my father was almost surely going to die. For a couple of seconds, I almost fainted. At the same time, my mother went into shock and I thought she was having a heart attack. Well, we took Mom to the emergency room and while she was lying there in shock, she said, "You know, if I'm going to be of any help to Dad, I'm going to have to get myself back together." And she did. She did it by prayer and again I saw the power that God can give us.

When the doctor asked if we wanted Dad to know how sick he was, Mom said, "I don't think he's strong enough." But I said, "Well, I'm going to vote that we tell him." Of course, I was elected to break the news! Now my father and I had a very powerful and warm relationship—just as much like two brothers as like father and son. How do you tell someone you love very much that he's dying?

Dad didn't say much. At that time, he didn't have a really meaningful relationship with God, but through the prayers of a lot of people and through a lot of conversations he began to realize that, even though he had not been close to God through his life, God loved him and wanted to support him during his time of need. Then Dad faced another problem—that of not being able to pray. He would lie in bed with such frustration because he couldn't pray that he would cry. It was a very difficult experience for everyone around. A young minister took an interest in Dad and started to visit him often. Between them, they built a tremendous bond. One day, although it was a very simple prayer—some might even call it shallow—Dad did learn to talk to God and bit by bit his prayers began to develop.

During this time, because the cancer had spread to Dad's spinal column, he began to experience a great deal of pain, but never once during this whole period did he lose his sense of humor or complain about what he was going through.

On November 23rd my father died. After the funeral service, the minister said, "You know, Bob, this is what I do for a living. I bury a lot of people and most of the services are like wakes; there is a great deal of sadness. But this service has been a victory celebration. Your father was able to meet this thing and in such a style that he came into a living relationship with God and gained strength from it. To see that and also to observe how this experience has noticeably affected the lives of your mother and sister —and not only their lives, but mine also—all this has made

watching and sharing the life of your father a very significant experience."

When people ask me how I feel about my father's death
and I tell them that it was a very powerful, very positive
event, they look at me as if they think I must be crazy, or as
if maybe I didn't love my father. What they don't realize is
that, first of all, when Dad could have died crying and full
of fear, he was supported, he had help when he needed it
and he was able to deal with death in a very powerful and
positive way. Besides, there were at least six people who
were very strongly affected by the life and the power that
Dad showed prior to his death. Dad made me see that God
is love, that He can give us power and that He can use
even a very bad situation to positively affect the lives of
people. Those are the reasons, then, that I can say the
death of my father was a positive and exciting experience,
even though I still miss him a great deal.

Another opportunity I've had to see the relevancy and
power of faith is within the business community. A couple
of years ago I started my own business. There have been
ups and downs, and it seems that there have been a lot
more downs than ups. Yet no matter how bleak things get,
I always have the possibility of looking to God and gaining strength from Him. I have quite a few people working
for me. They have problems. I see the kind of things that
happen in their lives and I try to help them. I find that the
business community offers the Christian a great platform
for witnessing and sharing his faith. Whether or not the
business will succeed, I don't know. But one thing has impressed me: whenever I've had a time of real deep need
God has been there to support me and give me encourage-
ment.

One concept of the Christian is that he is weak, lacking

substance, not really very vigorous—in fact, just not quite what a man ought to be. But that picture doesn't jibe with examples I've seen in my life as a professional athlete, in the business community and in the little town where I live. Many times I've seen a Christian confronted by a death in the family, a business going sour, or some other major calamity, and he hangs in there. He may be hurt, but he's not defeated. That's because he has a source of strength to turn to. Very frequently, in times of national emergencies when people who can be counted on are needed for service, in the vanguard of the people who are helping, giving of themselves, are the Christians. People can say what they want about Christians, but I know men and women who are more than willing to share their money, their time, their life, their family, their house—in fact, anything they have—with another person. This, to me, is a very exciting approach to life.

So many of the people who are hip, really cool dudes in society, go on drugs or something when things start happening to them, because they can't face life by themselves. They may look at a Christian's life and say, "Boy, he is really messing this thing up." What they don't realize is that the Christian is going to hang in there and fight and scratch and dig out. He's going to get on the right frequency with God and find out what God's will is for this particular problem and together he and God are going to fight the thing out. There won't be any drugs involved; there won't be any outside influences, because when he and God are right, that's all he needs.

I believe the thing that makes it so difficult for people to have access to this power and this relevancy of the Christian faith is the fact that it's so simple. So many of the things that we're involved with in life are complicated; it's difficult for people to begin realizing that there is a source of power available simply by asking for it. It costs no money. There is nothing you can do to earn it. It's just a very simple thing, saying, "God, my life isn't what I'd like it to be. I'm unhappy with who I am and what I stand for. I want to be a different person. I want to have a power that I don't have right now. I want to have a light shine out of me so that people can see You within my life. God, I want to have the selflessness to be able to feel more concern about my brother than about myself. I want to be able, to the best of my ability, to do Your will in my life." That's all it takes—just a very simple profession of faith, a simple request made in trust. In this way a person can gain power sufficient for all his needs in life. God has an answer for all of the day-to-day problems which confront us. We don't have to go to some sort of special text. We don't have to see a psychiatrist or a doctor or fight the problem all by ourselves. God works today. And most important, He *wants* to help us.

Lem Barney

LEM BARNEY   Cornerback   Detroit Lions

6 feet   188 pounds   Age—26
Jackson State College

Lem, now in his sixth year of pro ball, was All-Conference for three years as a collegiate defensive back. He averaged 41.6 yards as a college punter and in 1967 was a starter in the Blue-Gray game.

Lem is a daring defensive back and a constant threat to the opposition. In five seasons, he has accounted for 2,938 yards on kick-off and punt returns, scoring ten touchdowns. He was named NFL defensive Rookie-of-the-Year in 1967 and was voted All-Pro and Pro-Bowl honors in 1968 and 1969.

Lem and his wife, Martha, have one child and are full-time residents of Detroit.

LEM BARNEY
DETROIT LIONS—CORNERBACK

It was a nationally televised coast-to-coast football game
on a Sunday afternoon with millions of people watching.
The opposing team stopped, watched the ball—as did
the Detroit players.

>All of a sudden number 20—Lem Barney—edged
>toward the ball,
>picked it up
>and ran through the opposing team for a 71-yard
>touchdown!

It took knowledge to realize that it was a live football.
But it took courage to pick it up and run with it.

Lem Barney is the only person I know who, in his first
year of pro football was

>Rookie-of-the-Year
>as well as All-Pro at cornerback.

This shows ability. But the confidence from which his
ability grows is the courage Lem has in himself—

>not only as a football player,
>but as a person
>and as a Christian.

It takes courage to witness for Christ,
>to one person in a veterans hospital
>or to 5,000 young people at a Youth for Christ con-
>vention.

I have seen Lem Barney put this courage in action in
sharing his faith in Jesus Christ with his fellow athletes—

>with young people—
>and, in fact, wherever Christ leads him.

7

COURAGE

LEM BARNEY

Every man today is faced with the need for the kind of courage that will give him confidence in himself, and there are times in life when we all must realize that nothing is more valuable. I consider this kind of courage the first human quality, because it is the quality which makes it possible to acquire all others. In my chosen profession, which is football, I have to have confidence in myself and my ability every time I hit the field.

When I was a kid my mom and dad tried to instill this quality in me. But just as all of us at one time or another have been told something we didn't think was important at the time, it didn't make much of an impression then. Later on in life, though, I came to realize that I was being confronted with things they had talked about earlier, and now, as I said, the confidence that comes from courage is one of the most valuable things I could ever look for in life.

Courage that gives a person confidence is a great thing. One of my favorite quotes on courage is from Victor Hugo: "Have courage for the great sorrows of life and patience for the small ones. And when you have lavishly accomplished your daily tasks, go to sleep in peace. God is awake." I think this tells us a lot, not just about having courage in doing our daily tasks, but about having courage for larger problems as well. No matter what you do or how you do it, God is always there with an open eye. I don't think anyone can function without courage today. When you accomplish anything it is not just through freak accidents or being lucky. You have to believe in yourself first of all, because if you don't no one else will. Belief in yourself, along with the courage to act on your belief, helps with anything you want to acquire or hold onto—health, wealth, even life itself.

In my late teens I thought I was really at the crossroads, where I had to choose one way or the other, the right or the wrong, without really knowing how to find the right road. There's no way to tell where I might have ended up, and where I might be today, if I hadn't had courage, along with confidence in myself, advice and help from a great family and faith and trust in God.

All along the line in my life, at times when I was slacking off, there have been people who were ready to reach back and give me a helping hand. I really appreciate the fact that they were so amiable, because no one really has to help anyone if he chooses not to. Each man lives his own life. Just the same, when I needed help I've always been able to find it, sometimes outside the family and sometimes within the family circle. I have tried to carry this over in my own attitude toward others, because I believe that no matter how big, how wealthy, or how successful you get there is always room to share and to help others. I think that throughout my days thus far I can honestly say that whenever I was called on to do things, whether it was for an organization or a personal friend—any time I have seen a chance to help a brother—I would do so. It makes you feel real good at night to know that you have been able to lend a helping hand. I think this is what it is all about today —helping others and being helped in return.

When I was in high school I enjoyed singing in the choir during church and Sunday school, and also in the choral group at my school. But of all the songs I knew during my so-called singing days, the only one that has really stuck in my mind, the only one that stayed with me through all my growing up, was "Others," and it went like this:

> Lord, help me live from day to day,
> In such a self-forgetful way,
> That even when I kneel to pray,
> My prayers shall be for others.
>
> Others, Lord, yes, others,
> Let this my motto be:
> Help me to live for others,
> That I might live like thee.
>
> And when on earth my work is done
> And my new work in heaven's begun,
> May I forget the crown I've won,
> While thinking still of others.
>
> CHARLES M. MEIGS

There are more lyrics, but I just want to bring out that much because it expresses the fact that a person can try to live for others as the Master lived for us all. My family used to sing that hymn some nights just before having prayer. My family has always tried to carry on a Christian life and I think the most glorious thing in life is to be a

Christian. It's truly great, you know, that a person can have fellowship with God and really trust and believe on His Holy Word. I think it was Cicero, one of the world's greatest philosophers, who once said that a man of courage is also full of faith. It just goes to prove that you really can't have one without the other.

In one period of my collegiate days it seemed that somehow I'd gotten further from Christ, or that Christ was no longer with me. I tried to remember that once you invite Christ into your heart He is there to stay. I kept trying to reason with myself and to find out why I did not feel fulfilled as much as before about having Christ. I still continued to go to church; I continued reading the Bible; but somehow I just felt like an empty void. Later on, about my senior year in college, I started feeling better, even though I was doing nothing different.

After being drafted by the Lions in '67, I think that one of the best things that ever happened to me was to meet a guy by the name of Dr. Ira Lee Eshleman. Dr. Eshleman set up some of the players' chapel services in pro football. This gave me a chance for a new experience with the guys I was with every day—guys I lived and died with every day through meetings, practice and then the game on Saturday or Sunday. Every Sunday we'd have a different person come in and share with us his beliefs and how he came to know Christ on a personal basis. This was especially good for me because I couldn't get a chance to go to a church service. The team had to be at the stadium at 11 o'clock or 11:30. The guys who were Catholic could get up and go to mass, but normally if you were a Baptist, or a Methodist, like I am, you had to miss church. I think these sessions were one of the most fantastic things that happened to me in my entire life because, at a time when I thought maybe I would again grow away from Christ, they brought me closer to Him.

And I think another of the greatest things that happened to me was in 1971, when I went to a four-day seminar for Christian athletes down in Dallas, Texas. I can really say they were four of the most enjoyable days of my life, because I had a chance to give my testimony and hear the testimonies of other ball players. On the last day there we were called on to go out to various communities and share and pray with others and for others. I've always been one for prayers, but I had never had the opportunity until then to pray for others. I must admit that it was a strange and different feeling. But it was like the old cliché, "It was really no hill for a stepper," because I had it, it was just bubbling inside me and from then on it was easy—just like greeting someone with "Hello," "Good morning," or "How are you?"

At that meeting I was introduced to the four spiritual laws. These four spiritual laws, as written by Dr. Bill Bright, president and founder of the Campus Crusade for Christ International, are, basically: (1) God *loves* you and has a wonderful *plan* for your life. (2) Man is *sinful* and *separated* from God, thus he cannot know and experience God's love and plan for his life. (3) Jesus Christ is God's *only* provision for man's sin. Through Him you can know and experience God's love and plan for your life. (4) We must individually *receive* Jesus Christ as Saviour and Lord; then we can know and experience God's love and plan for our lives. When I got back from Dallas, the first thing I asked my wife was the test that we were taught to give, to find out if she had heard the four spiritual laws. She hadn't, so I had a chance to really expound and experiment with her. I'm happy to say that my wife is a Christian and I think we have a beautiful Christian family. A family without Christ is just a mere existing family. It's not a family on top. I like to consider my family as being a top family.

While we were down in Dallas at the seminar I had an opportunity to go over the four spiritual laws with a group of high-school kids. After reading and going through the laws, I gave them cards and pencils and told them to be truthful and secretly write down whether they accepted Christ. Out of the fifteen guys in my group, fourteen accepted.

I must truthfully admit that before going to Dallas I thought that if you prayed for others and were outgoing in a Christian way your friends who had not accepted Christ and did not have a Christlike life would look at you differently. But after that it really didn't matter how a friend felt, because I felt it was my position to tell him my way of thinking toward Christ and to really try to win him over to my side. Most of the ones I went over the four spiritual laws with know my side now, so it's like having a couple of new recruits in our brigade.

Also, I had an opportunity to give a testament and read the four spiritual laws to a group of about 600 or 700 people up in Flint, Michigan, for a prayer breakfast put on by the city's mayor. I took along several packs of the four spiritual laws and when the breakfast was over they were all gone. I even received letters shortly thereafter, from others who had been there, requesting more copies of the four spiritual laws.

Getting back to the subject of confidence and courage, there are some beautiful quotes. One of them goes like this: "We must have courage to bet on our ideas, to take the calculated risk and to act. Everyday living requires courage if life is to be effective and bring happiness." That is from Maxwell Maltz. I think you can find the most famous quotes ever in the daily book—the Bible. One of my favorites tells us: "Be strong and of a good courage, fear not, nor be afraid of them: for the Lord thy God, he it is that doth go with thee; he will not fail thee, nor forsake thee" (Deuteronomy 31:6).

I remember a quote by A. P. Gulf saying that Jesus Christ never did any of the things that usually accompany greatness. He wrote no books. He never held public office. He was no world traveler, explorer or investor. He never owned his own home, had a family or founded a business. As a public figure, popular opinion was against Him. Finally He died like a criminal and was buried like a pauper, but the passing centuries have marked Him as the greatest of the great. His name is in the thoughts and on the lips of men everywhere. His way of life has always been man's highest hope of best living. It is now his only hope of survival. We shall either take His way or there is no way.

That is beautiful. I pray that God will give us all the courage and confidence to find His way and to take it throughout our lives.

Norm Evans

NORM EVANS   Offensive Tackle   Miami Dolphins

6 feet 5 inches   252 pounds   Age—29
Texas Christian University

Norm played offensive tackle and defensive end at TCU and captained the team his senior year. He was drafted by Houston and played for one year before going to Miami in 1966. He served as offensive captain for the Dolphins in 1967. Twice chosen as Miami's best offensive linesman, he was one of the prime factors in the Dolphins' winning of the AFC championship which put them in Super Bowl VI. In 1971, he was named to UPI's All-AFC squad.

Norm and his wife, Bobbie, have a son, Ron, and a daughter, Deana. They live in Hollywood, Florida, where Norm, during the off season, works as national account representative for Ryder Truck Lines.

NORM EVANS
MIAMI DOLPHINS—OFFENSIVE TACKLE

The Apostle Paul said,
> "For I determined not to know any thing among you,
> save Jesus Christ, and him crucified" (1 Corinthians
> 2:2).

This was determination and that is obvious in the life of
Norm Evans. He is

> a determined football player,
> a determined husband,
> a determined father.

But I think above all else, he has a determination to live
his life for Jesus Christ.

For all the determination, Norm Evans still takes time
to pray about every matter that comes into his life. I will
never forget the afternoon I saw Norm Evans with another
member of the football team,

> standing in a corner of the room,
> arms around each other,
> asking God to help this other player with a particular
> problem in his life.

Determined? Yes!
But his confidence is in the Christ
> whom he loves so much—
> whom he lives for so well!

8

DETERMINATION

NORM EVANS

If I had to choose one word as a basis for my thoughts about my life up to now, that word would be determination, because determination has always been one of my strongest characteristics.

I have to admit that my determination wasn't always the best thing for me. We lived on a dairy farm, and I had certain chores that were part of my requirement—cleaning the barn and feeding the chickens and gathering the eggs, and that sort of thing—but I was determined to do as little as possible. I always goofed off, and my dad would have to tell me over and over to do my work. Then my determination not to do it would get me in trouble, because Dad would end up having to motivate me with his belt. That is just one of the ways my determination brought me grief from my earliest memories.

My dad used to talk about the pet squirrel he had when he was a boy, and what a great time he had with it. He had kept it in a cage on the porch, and sometimes he would let it run in the house. It had been a joy in his life. In fact, it was a dear pet to the whole family. When I was about four years old I was determined to follow Dad's example and have a pet squirrel of my own. We lived at the time in Santa Fe, New Mexico, where there were quite a few squirrels and chipmunks, and also some large striped lizards, which were known as rainbow lizards, I believe. My mother tells the story that one day I came running in from outside yelling, "Ma, Ma, I finally caught that pet squirrel!" When she came to look, she nearly fainted: I was holding a huge striped lizard by the tail!

My determination to have a pet squirrel did nothing but scare my mother half to death, and she assured me that I'd never have a pet squirrel of that particular color and type. And so one of my first memories of determination in my life ended in disaster.

Another instance that almost got me into serious trouble was my determination to have the best turtle collection in the neighborhood. One of my favorite places to hunt for turtles was in a creek not far from our house. However, there were snakes around the creek and Dad had issued an order to stay away. He was thinking of my well-being, of course, but I was determined, so I'd go down and wade in the creek and catch turtles. One day I was bitten by a snake. I remember my mother rushing me to the doctor, and the tourniquet, and the whole bit—quite a traumatic experience. Although I didn't realize it at the time, my hardheadedness—or call it determination—once more had gotten me into trouble.

The next recollection is my first encounter with a coach, in junior high school. I was big for my age, and the coach wanted me out for athletics. He was one of the old-school, hard-nosed coaches who enjoyed motivating the boys with a paddle, and because of my determination not to be pushed around by anyone or "encouraged" by paddling,

I determined that I would not be on his teams. As a result it seemed that every time I turned around I was in trouble, having to run extra laps or getting a couple of licks with the paddle. So in this encounter, once again, my determination caused problems for me. I spent my entire junior high school career regretting that determination because I always seemed to be in trouble with that particular coach.

Then I went to high school. Since it was a different school and a different coach, and since all my friends were involved in athletics, I was determined to get in there and play, too. On the first day of football practice, I didn't even know how to put on the uniform. Several of the guys had to show me, but I was still determined. In practice, I can remember the head-on blocking and going through the drills, learning how to do the exercises. It seems silly now to realize that there was a time when I didn't know how to do these things, but I recall vividly how embarrassed and troubled I was because I didn't understand or didn't know how to do them and all the other guys did.

This time determination paid off for me; within a month I was in the starting lineup of the varsity football team. However, it also got me into trouble, because even though I was determined to play I was still Mama's boy, I guess. I had an injury to my back, and the doctor told me it was nothing except a slight muscle pull. But I determined it was a severe injury. I was pulling up in practice because I thought I was hurt. My coach, Jim Easly, took me aside and said, "Norm, this isn't a boy's game. This is a man's game. If you're going to play, you'll have to resolve that you'll play sometimes when it's not comfortable for you to play. You're going to play when you're tired, and you're going to play when maybe you have a little ache or pain here or there." I remember he walked me in that day, even while practice was still going. "You sit in here, and you think about it," he told me. "Do you really want to play this game, or are you just out here to mess around with the boys? You make up your mind. Determine whether you want to play the game. Then you come tell me, and we'll go on from there."

So again I had to determine what I wanted to do. Amazingly, my back injury got well overnight, because I determined that the man was right. If I wanted to play, I was really going to have to give it all I had. So that was what I determined in my mind to do. I resolved from that day on that I'd do everything I possibly could to be the player Coach Easly wanted me to be. I worked hard and was successful.

The same thing was true when I was in college. I was determined. Even though I was somewhat small for a college lineman—weightwise, at least—I decided that I'd just outfight anybody for the job. And I did it adequately, I guess, because I was drafted by the pros.

I remember, through these high school and college years, I determined in my own mind that I wanted to be a Christian—but I wanted to make my own rules. Just like when I was a child my determination got me into trouble because I wanted to do it my way, I wanted to meet God on *my* terms. So I determined what I thought it would take to be a Christian. I believed that all I would have to do would be to go to church, to do God a favor occasionally. I knew some Bible stories; that ought to help, I thought. Then, if I gave a dollar here and there I decided I would be doing my part. As a result I was nothing but a very frustrated person.

I determined that I was going to read the Bible, and I'd read for a day or two and then put it down in frustration. I determined that I would pray and have a time to myself, because I heard a pastor say that was what Christians should do. Again I was frustrated; I wasn't able to maintain my study because it didn't interest me. As a matter of fact, it was a chore, like working out. I was determined that my wife should go to church with me. But she and I are from different backgrounds, and didn't see eye-to-eye on some things, such as which church we should attend. As a result my determination along that line led only to more frustration and problems.

I remember when I was drafted into pro football, how hard I worked. I was determined to make it because I'd been challenged: one of my coaches had said I could never succeed in pro ball because I didn't have the temperament. So I determined that I *would* make it. When I started working out, I lifted weights three days a week, for three or four hours a day. I ran sprints—twenty fifty-yard sprints every single day, and played handball probably six or seven hours a week. As a result, when I got to training camp I was in great condition. You see, I had to set my mind: I was determined that if I just made it in pro ball I'd have the world by the tail; I wouldn't ever need anything else. As a result of determination and hard work, I got into pro football, and I thought I had it made because I was a starter as a rookie on the Houston team.

I was determined to settle down in Houston, but bingo! As soon as the season was over, I discovered I'd been traded to the Miami Dolphins. That really upset me, because I had my heart set on playing in Texas, for the Oilers. But as time wore on, I decided that if Houston didn't care any more than that about me, I was going to get out of that place. So I left Texas early, before training camp, and went to the Dolphin training camp, knowing that I was going to be just like a rookie again. That's one thing that disturbed me; I didn't like all the struggle that was involved, but I knew that everyone would be a rookie in Miami, and I was determined to make the club. I worked hard.

It was along about this time that I made a discovery: even though I had made the club, my life was empty. I always wanted my life to count for something; I always wanted it to be worthwhile; and now, I discovered the cause of my frustration in life—my poor, ineffectual attempt to be a Christian.

One night I went to hear the chaplain of Bourbon Street, Bob Harrington, speak. All of a sudden it became clear to me that the reason I was so frustrated, the reason I was having such a hard time—even though I was determined to be what God wanted me to be—was that I was trying to do it on my own terms. I realized that God loved me, as an individual, very much. He loved me to the point that He had sent His son, Jesus Christ, into this world to die for me because I was a sinner. I couldn't save myself. I had done things wrong. I'd rebelled against God. I could never be a Christian until I was willing to say, "Okay, God, I know I can't do it on my own power; I can't be in Your family by determining I *want* to be in it unless I'm willing to go a step further, and let You control my determination." That night I asked Jesus Christ to come into my life and take control. I asked Him to forgive me for the things that I'd done wrong, and He did.

When Jesus came into my life, for the first time my determination to be what God wanted me to be found purpose and meaning. I realized that, even though as a child I had many determinations, and I'd always been headstrong and set my mind on certain things, most of the time determination can cause problems for you. True, it's great in working for success, but I found that my success only brought me emptiness, because I wanted my life to count for something. Here I was, I had made it at pro ball that first year in Houston. I woke up one day and realized I had more money, better clothes, a nicer apartment, a new car—all these things, but still my life was empty. And I was working so hard for accomplishment; I was so determined to be successful. I couldn't understand why I wasn't, and then I realized what I lacked. It wasn't my determination that was lacking, it was the power in my life. It was the depth. It was *God*. God in His Son, Jesus Christ. And so, when I finally came to the point where I realized that determination wasn't enough, I had to have Jesus in my life. Then I began to understand what real determination was.

It has been interesting to see how my determination about things like Bible study and prayer life have changed since I asked Christ to come into my life. I now find that it's thrilling to search God's Word. There are so many promises in it for us that we can claim if we believe them and determine to allow Christ to control our lives. God's promises of wisdom and love and assurance are priceless to me. It excites me to know that God is with us no matter how difficult the situation, and to see that all things do work together for good when we love God and are called according to His purpose.

My prayer life has become a wonderful part of my life— such an exciting adventure. I've determined to try to pray about everything. Many times Satan says, "Hey, what do you need to talk to God about that for?" In spite of that, it's thrilling to see God work in my life. Since I'm determined to allow God to do what He will with me, I get up in the morning excited about "Well, God, what's going to happen today?" I ask Him to be in control of my life and entrust the day to Him. I know that He will make us adequate if only we're available to Him. So I've determined in my life to be available to God, and not to live under my own power or in my own determination, but in the power of the Holy Spirit to be what God wants me to be. I have discovered that I'm a better athlete because of Jesus Christ in my life. I now realize that my labors should be as it says in Colossians 3:17 and 3:23, 24—that it's the Lord I'm working for. All the ability that I have is given to me by Him, and so I should determine to do what I can for Him.

Before I came to Jesus, I determined that in my marriage things were going to be done my way. My wife and I have known each other since we were in grade school, and we went together all during high school. We were married very young, and I just determined that I was going to be boss. If I decided to go fishing or whatever, I just did it. I didn't really concern myself with how she felt about it. This created some terrible problems, as you can imagine. We were in a constant state of upheaval, and we had a continuous war going on. We'd have one good day and two bad ones, and because I was hardheaded, I wouldn't give in. I had to have things my way, and so once again my determination got me into trouble.

However, that was before I finally realized the problem of my Christian life: that I hadn't trusted Christ—I hadn't really turned my life over to Him. I was just trying to be a Christian under my own steam. On the same night that I asked Christ to come into my life, Bobbie, my wife, also asked Him to come into hers. And so, finally, we made it. We had something in common; we had Jesus in our lives.

And what a difference it has made, because now we've determined to have our family conform to what Christ wants, to what the Bible teaches a family should be.

My wife lets me be the leader in our house, and I'm just bound and determined to let Christ be boss in my life. As my wife and I have grown closer to God and allowed Christ, the power of God, and the Holy Spirit into our lives, we've found that we're closer to each other. The more we let God empower and control our lives, the closer we become, and I can truthfully say now that my wife is my best friend. It's hard to believe that there was a time when I wondered how much longer we could last at the rate we were going, simply because I was determined to have things my way.

How grateful I am to have discovered that determination can be channeled to be something worthwhile rather than just a source of frustration. I've found that no matter how successful you are before you find Christ—or before He finds you—your determination channeled by God can be something much more worthwhile and meaningful. God can put purpose in your life when you can't do it yourself, no matter how much you accomplish by your own determination. I have to be quite determined as an athlete because I face Bubba Smith, Deacon Jones, Carl Eller, Gerry Philbin, Rich Jackson, Claude Humphrey—all the real fine athletes around the league. The majority of them outweigh me, and are probably faster than I am. But I am determined. This has always been the key to my success as an athlete.

And now I've begun to play for God. I realize that every ability that I have comes to me as a blessing from Him, so I've determined, now that I'm a Christian, to give God the glory, or try to give God the glory, for every success

I have. Truly, my successes are gifts from Him, because He has given me the ability and the opportunity to play.

It amazes me to see the difference that Christ has made in my life. When I used to be so frustrated, if I missed a play I'd have sleepless nights over it. But I have peace now because I go into the game better prepared—prepared not only physically, but spiritually as well. I've never prayed for superstrength or ability beyond what God has given me; I simply ask Him to give me the concentration and to guide my determination to do the best I can. It has been exciting for me to experience the peace I've had about the way I've played and to see the success I've had.

I've encountered some difficulties, of course. When I had an injury a few years ago, how grateful I was that I was God's man, because I don't have to be an athlete now to be a success. In fact, I don't have to be anything in particular to be a success, except God's man. In the face of injury, I claim Romans 8:28: ". . . all things work together for good to them that love God, to them who are the called according to his purpose."

In the chaotic business of pro football, I claim God's word and find peace in my life—even in the midst of pressure from every side, both physically and mentally. The strain on a winning team is almost unbearable, and I wonder how some guys play without God in their lives. I don't believe I could stand it. In fact, I don't understand how anyone can go on under the strain of everyday life without Christ, no matter how determined he is. From my experience, it seems that the more determined you are, the more frustrated you get when you still have that emptiness and that groping in your life because you haven't found Christ.

So now my prime determination is not in the direction of athletics, but in the direction of being what God wants me to be. I'm determined to be available to God, to let Him use me in whatever way He wants. I believe that this is the most important thing as far as I'm concerned, and as long as I walk determined to be what God wants me to be, I can have peace of mind that I could never have any other way. I've discovered that God can use me, and this is what I think is so exciting about my life. God has let me be a part of His work because I'm available. He's allowed me to help others come to know Him in a personal way. Now this is not because of anything I've done, but because God allows us all, if we will, to be a part of His plan.

I'm not only determined to be the best athlete I can possibly be, but I'm also bound and determined to be the kind of dad and the kind of husband He wants me to be. I'm determined to try to be the kind of man God wants me to be. I'm determined to try to learn as much as I can about the Lord I serve. For so long I was such an authority on something I was completely ignorant about, but now I'm going to try to study God's Word more and spend more time in prayer. And I've determined to try to be available at every opportunity God can find for using me. I've learned that it's not my ability that God wants—He just wants me to be available.

So I guess you can say I've got a new set of determinations all the way around. They're all motivated by the fact that God loves me. He has given me any abilities I have. In fact, every breath of my life comes from Him. So now I've dedicated my determination to Him. I'm so glad I've finally discovered that although we can be successful materially and as far as society is concerned by being determined, hard-working people, we can only be enthusiastically determined if we put God first in our lives. God plus enthusiasm and determination equals a success that the world can never measure. I'm so grateful to God that He has become the center of my family and of my life, because now I can be the type of athlete I was created to be and the type of man I was created to be—not because of my determination, but because of what Jesus Christ has done in my life and what a difference He has made.

Charley Harraway

CHARLEY HARRAWAY   Running Back
                                    Washington Redskins
6 feet 2 inches   215 pounds   Age—28
San Jose State College

Charley, now in his seventh season of pro ball, set college records for scoring, most carries for season, longest run from scrimmage and most yards rushing in one game. During his senior year, he scored 14 touchdowns to tie Heisman Trophy winner Mike Garrett for Pacific Coast Conference scoring lead. He played in the East-West and Hula Bowl games.

Last season he carried the ball 146 times for 577 yards and caught twenty-four passes for a total offensive yardage of 713 to make him the eleventh leading rusher in the AFC.

Charley and his wife, Gail, have one son and live in Silver Springs, Maryland.

CHARLEY HARRAWAY
WASHINGTON REDSKINS—RUNNING BACK

John says, ". . . God is love" (1 John 4:8).
    God's love is the origin of our salvation in Christ.
Charley Harraway recently experienced that love for himself by an act of faith in Christ. The first time I heard Charley speak publicly,
    that love came through.
    That love came through in his face—
    that love came through in his actions—
    that love came through in what he said.
In spite of a year of injury and frustration, Charley Harraway has learned

        to share that love—
        to spread that love to other people.

    Not only is love the origin of our salvation, it is the heart of our witnessing for Christ.

        To know about love theoretically is one thing:
        To live love practically is something else.

The love he tells about here
    is the love that Charley Harraway lives.

9

LOVE

CHARLEY HARRAWAY

Have you ever wondered who you are? How you came about? When the beginning actually was? When the end will be?

Have you ever wondered who was in the beginning? If there was a beginning? I have, and I still wonder, but my mind leads me to believe that in the beginning there was a Creator. I'm not able to comprehend the beginning before man began. When I talk about the beginning, I mean the beginning of mankind, because our scientists tell us that in the beginning a creature came out of the sea and that he evolved into man as we know him today. But if this is true, where did the creature come from? If it is true, how was the pattern laid out for him to evolve into what man is today?

As intelligent human beings, how can we begin to believe that the creature of that time could have survived, had the intelligence to adapt to conditions as they were then and come along to what man is today? How can we accept that when we see here, today, all of our own limitations? In our supposedly superintelligent age, we think

111

of ourselves as brilliant in comparison to the creatures that existed in the ages before and after the dinosaur. If we are brilliant, as we profess to be, how can we accept the fact that the animal from which man is supposed to have sprung has evolved into man as we know him? I, for one, can't accept that. I could accept it, though, if you could show me that a pattern had been laid out for the evolution of mankind by someone far more intelligent than man.

I can envision, in the beginning, this one dude, peering down upon whatever there was to peer down upon at the time. I can envision a master plan forming in his mind. And of course, with any creation, you never start out with the ultimate, so I can envision this cat outlining a format. Of course, he knew what the end result would be. But I can envision that format being laid out, let's say in the way that scientists have supposedly traced man's evolution backwards to the beginning of man from the seas. I can envision his plans all ready in that fashion, just as a baby is born. Before it begins to do anything else, it cries, and then its hands and feet begin to move and then one day it begins to crawl and then to utter words. Then it begins to walk, not realizing all the time that its mind is beginning to function and develop and mature as it goes into the years.

I can accept a plan like this and I can accept it for the evolution of mankind, but what I can't accept is the feeling that's shared so widely throughout the world that man just came about and that there was no creator—that man simply emerged, just accidentally, or whatever. My feeling is that there was a plan for man, just as parents today plan to have children. And I feel that the love that we have today for our children is indicative of the love of the Being who had the plan for man.

Can you imagine parents planning for a child and then, after having it, not caring for it, not looking out for it, not making sure, whenever danger arises, that they are there to protect it? I think this love of parent for child was all in the plans of God when He created man. I feel that you can directly relate the love man has for his children to the love God has for man. There are so many things God has given us, feelings related to Him that we aren't able to grasp fully, but the love we have for our children is one thing linking us to God that we can really understand. The love we have for our children is probably the most unselfish love man knows.

Let's take the family as a whole. Consider the husband's love for his wife, how it all came about and where it is today. It initially evolved out of an emotional feeling, a sexual feeling. It developed as it grew, but the reason it developed, more than anything else, was that the husband —or the wife, for that matter—wanted to be loved. It developed as a need rather than as a concept of giving. We like to think that we love because we want to make another person feel wanted, but really, as selfish as we are, we love because *we* want to feel wanted, we want our love returned.

And now let's look at the child's love toward the parents. The child loves his parents because they love him. Since his beginning they have taken care of his needs and desires. They have protected him when he was in danger; fed him when he was hungry. The child's love is basically selfish. But when we look at the parents' love for the child the picture is quite different. There is nothing the child can do for his parents; there is no sexual motivation involved. In the beginning, the parents love the child because he is a creation of theirs. That love grows throughout the child's life. The parents protect the child from the moment of birth until he leaves home. And when he is mature, they still worry about him, even when they can no longer help him. Just as with everything else, this love we have for our children came from God, and just as with everything else that we have derived from God, it is diminished tremendously in comparison with the love He has for us. We've only been given, or were able to receive, a small measure of His attributes.

Let us suppose that you're living in a real nice $50,000 home. You have a couple of cars in the garage. Let's say that you also have a four- or five-year-old child. You're lying back in front of your color television set, enjoying all the nice modern conveniences that you have. And now let's say that someone enters your home and tells you he's going to take everything you have.

Then he tells you that he'll leave you one thing. Whatever you want most out of all those things, he'll spare you. What will you say? I've learned, through my three-year-old son, that if I could be spared only one thing, I would say, "Spare my son." I think that's the general feeling among loving parents.

Some two thousands years ago, God was looking down on the world, and He saw how troubled it was. I think He felt just as we feel after our kids leave home. "They're in great need," He must have thought. "I wish there were something I could do, some way I could show them how much I love them." And at that time He thought about the love that we have for our children. That must have been when He decided to send His Son, His only-begotten Son, Jesus Christ.

What's written in the Scriptures is that God loved the world so much that He gave His only-begotten Son, so that whoever believed in Him should not perish, but have eternal life. This is what makes me begin to realize how much we're loved by God, because I personally can't conceive of giving my son's life for anything. I can think of nothing that I would want enough to make that sacrifice. But God gave His Son for us. So you see, since I would give my life to save my son, this makes me know that God loves me even more than I love myself: He gave His Son's life to save me and all mankind, whereas I could not give my son's life to save my own.

And how about the Son of God, Jesus Christ? What type of man was He? Before His crucifixion, Jesus had been quoted in the Scriptures as saying, ". . . Love your enemies, bless them that curse you, do good to them that hate you, and pray for them which despitefully use you, and persecute you; That ye may be the children of your Father which is in heaven . . ." (Matthew 5:44, 45). We all know what happened to Jesus Christ on the day of His crucifixion, how He was stripped and beaten, how they jammed a thorny crown onto His head and proceeded to lift a heavy wooden cross onto His back and make Him carry it. And then, spitting on Him, kicking Him, laughing at Him, they nailed Him to that cross.

I remember when I was a kid, I used to wonder, "Man, if this cat is as powerful as they say He is, why didn't He just zap them?" I remember not having much faith in Him, thinking that if He was who He said He was, He would have taken care of business right then. But now I'm able to comprehend what actually happened and why He didn't zap them that day. I understand the love that God has for us and I understand the mission He sent Jesus Christ on. Jesus Christ was sent to save all mankind from sin—all the sins that had ever been committed from the days of Adam right on up to today. He was sent as a sacrifice—a human sacrifice—and had He not followed through with the plans that were laid out for Him, mankind would have been doomed. Because remember, God said that whoever believed in Jesus Christ should have eternal life. So if Jesus had given up and not followed through with the plans, then there would be no eternal life. There wouldn't be any glory in heaven alongside God for any of us. Jesus Christ, shortly before He died, looked down upon the men who had beaten Him, who were spitting on Him and laughing at Him, and said, ". . . Father, forgive them; for they know not what they do" (Luke 23:34). This is the way Jesus lived and this is the way Jesus died, loving His enemies and praying for His persecutors, just as He had said all of God's children ought to do. He was willing to die because of the love that He has for mankind. Jesus said the great commandment is, ". . . Thou shalt love the Lord thy God with all thy heart, and with all thy soul, and with all thy mind." And the second is, ". . . Thou shalt love thy neighbor as thyself" (Matthew 22:37–39).

With all the hatred that we have in the world, we have to build on the message of Jesus, because He showed us how to live in the greatest sense.

Billy Zeoli

10

GOD'S GAME PLAN

BILLY ZEOLI

Now I want to sum up
>
> what has changed the lives of all the people in this
> book.
>
> what has given them forgiveness and freedom from
> guilt in the past.
>
> what has given them direction, purpose and meaning
> for life in the present.
>
> what has given them hope and confidence for the
> future.

These men are different—they stand out as individuals.

They have learned how to discover—and to follow—God's
plans for their lives.

What the Bible says, in its simplest and most condensed
form, is what God's game plan is all about. Put aside, if
you will, your preconceived thoughts about religion and
what you think the Bible says. For here, in a nutshell, is

GOD'S GAME PLAN.

Every football team always has a game plan, decided
well before the game between the coach and his staff and

then presented to the team. The team tries to follow this plan during the entire football game and they must play it by the rules put forth for the game of football.

In His rule book for life, called

the Bible

God presents His game plan in a very clear and expressive way. The first thing the Bible says is that there is a

problem:

God and man are separated by man's sin.
We have all kinds of definitions for this thing called *sin*. Romans 2:16 tells us it is simply missing God's mark or standard, which is Jesus Christ.

> For all have sinned, and come short of the glory of God (Romans 3:23).

> . . . the wages of sin is death . . . (Romans 6:23).

I remember a time in college. I was trying to explain how God and man are separated by man's sins. All of a sudden some pious Joe called out,

"I have never sinned!"

I was amazed and shocked. *Everyone* was shocked. I knew this was contrary to what God's Word said and tried to figure a way to show that he was like the rest of us.

Very quietly, I lifted my size 12E foot—and aimed it at his anklebone. Then, *with all of my might,* I came down against his instep. He bellowed out some choice swear words.

I said,

"Now you're a sinner like me.

Now we can talk.

Now you can listen to what God has to say to you."

Anyone trying to pretend that he is *not* a sinner is only faking himself out.

Man tries many ways to reach God,
but none of them can ever work.
One way is called the family plan.

Just because your father and mother are something, doesn't mean that you are going to be the same in any field—and being a child of God is no exception. The fact that your parents may be Christians in no way covers YOU. Remember, God has *no* grandchildren, only *children*.

Another way man tries to reach God is by the church route.

I am all for the church. I believe in the church. But too many people think that going to church can make them Christians. Now,
I have been in a lot of professional locker rooms,
I have put on lots of helmets and lots of gear,
I have tried on parts of uniforms,
I have held many footballs in my hands,
but, every time I walk out of a locker room, I am still the same nonathlete I was when I walked in. Going into that locker room cannot make me a football player—any more than going to church can make me a Christian!

Another way people try to get to heaven is by doing good.

We get our Christianity confused with the credit card system. There are credit cards for almost everything—but they don't work with God. God's Word says that even our righteousness is as filthy rags in His sight.

Still another way people try to get to God is by doing their own thing.

That seems to be very big today. The problem is

GOD ALREADY DID HIS THING

so for us to do our thing is contrary to His very will. The Bible says, "There is a way which seemeth right unto a man, but the end thereof are the ways of death" (Proverbs 14:12).

Yes! People try to do their own thing today, but that is *not* the way to God.

If the first thing the Bible tells us about is the problem that man and God are separated by sin, the second thing is the **answer.**

I remember, as a student, walking in skid row in Chicago, trying to share my faith with people and communicate the gospel of Christ. In talking with one man, I started to quote from John 3:16. I got as far as

For God so loved the world . . .

when he stopped me cold and finished the verse himself:

. . . that he gave his only begotten Son, that whosoever believeth in him should not perish, but have everlasting life.

Then he introduced himself. He was—**Ira Hayes**—the Indian who, with other men, planted the American flag on a hill of Iwo Jima during World War II. "They are building a bronze monument in our honor in Washington, D.C.," he told me.

"But, sir," I said, "in spite of that, you need to know Jesus Christ and John 3:16 tells what God wants you to do."

"You take your John 3:16 and get out of here," he shouted. He turned around and walked the other way.

I called after him, but he would not return. Three months later I saw an article in the *U.S. News and World Report* magazine titled

IWO JIMA HERO FOUND DEAD.

Ira Hayes had fallen,
   face down in a drunken stupor
      outside a taproom in Phoenix, Arizona, and
        had drowned
           in six inches of water
              too drunk to even turn his head.
That man refused to listen, but the solution I had offered him was the right one. Jesus Christ said, ". . . I am the way, the truth, and the life: no man cometh unto the Father, but by me" (John 14:6). We come to God through the person of Jesus Christ.

          That's the answer—
          the *only* answer.

Yes, Jesus Christ is God's answer to our problems. Yes, He can transform our lives.

In Los Angeles a few years ago, I visited a mission called *His Place,* where they try to share, with hippie kids and drug users, Jesus Christ. There I met a beautiful black man, about nineteen years old. To find out what the thing was all about, I played the devil's advocate a bit. He showed me
    some kids who were on drugs,
    some who were stoned,
    some with flasks of booze in their pockets,
    some trying to pop pills and
    some who were really way out of the whole scene.

When I asked what they were going to do with the kids,
he simply said,

"We're going to help them."
I asked how—and *he simply said,*

"We're going to feed them at midnight."
He explained,

"When we're finished feeding them, we are going to tell
them about Jesus Christ and how He can change their
lives. Christ can give them everlasting life and He can
also give them something for earth."

I asked,

"How can that possibly help them?"
Then, he told me,

"Nine months ago, I was sitting out there and this cat got
up and told about Jesus Christ, how He loved me and
would change my life if I would accept Him. I walked
and crawled down there and asked Christ to be my
Saviour."

I said,

"I guess you're going to tell me you're off drugs."

Then he really got firm. His eyes evidenced anger and he
answered,

"Listen, fella, I've had no problem with drugs for the last
nine months. Christ has helped me."

By now, I was crying. He wondered why, so I told him.

Forty-eight years ago, in Eastern State Penitentiary in
Philadelphia, there was a young Italian of twenty-two
who had been on drugs.
He had tried the drug cure—fifteen times!
Nothing had ever helped.

He was even smuggling in drugs and pushing them
in prison.

His list of charges was a mile long.

One day, someone threw a New Testament in his cell.
Looking at it, the first thing he saw was the Scripture
that says, "Heaven and earth shall pass away, but my
words shall not pass away" (Matthew 24:35).

He went out into the yard.

There he met a man carrying a Bible—a man who
had become a Christian in prison.

This man showed him how he could come to know
Jesus Christ.

That night, this Italian kid, who had already been in
jail six years of his life

knelt down in his cell and asked Christ to become his
Saviour.

When he left prison, he became an evangelist and he has
led thousands of people to Christ.

"I want to tell you, my friend, I *know* you can stay off
drugs!" I said,

"because that man,

the one off drugs for forty-eight years,

he's my father."

By now, *he* was crying. We felt ridiculous, both of us
there—crying together.

All of a sudden, my new friend said,

"You've got to help me get some peanut butter!"

When I asked what he wanted peanut butter for, he told
me that every night they fed the kids peanut butter and
bread. A Jewish baker donated the bread: each of the staff,
to which he belonged at that time, was responsible for
peanut butter on a different night.

This was his night.

Can you picture us? He on one side of the room—and me on the other—praying for peanut butter?

In the most beautiful and simple terms, he prayed something like this:
"God: We've got a problem!
I have to come up with peanut butter.
If I don't, I am going to be in trouble, 'cause all these kids now know that I'm on Your side.
And, by the way, if I don't come up with it, You won't look so good either."
Across the room, I was also beseeching God to do something about the peanut butter situation.
Suddenly,
I realized that the possible solution lay in my hands.
I pulled out my wallet and took out the only bill there.
I gave it to him.
I realized only then that it was a twenty.
He took the money, he looked up to heaven and he said with all of his heart,

"God, when You give peanut butter—
You really do give peanut butter!"

Now, all of us are not like my father and this man. But all of us, to some degree, have the problem of separation from God by our sin.

And the answer is Jesus Christ.

Since man could not reach to God,
God came down to us in the person of his son, Jesus Christ,
who was born of the Virgin Mary,
who died on the cross,

> who was buried,
> who arose again from the dead.

The third thing the Bible talks about is

decision!

Each of us has to make a decision concerning Jesus Christ. We've got to accept or reject God's plan for our lives. Simply, the Bible tells us that there are three possible answers.

> You can say *yes* to God.
> You can say *no* to God.
> You can say *maybe* to God.

If you say *yes*

you accept Jesus Christ into your heart as your personal Saviour. You say to Him, "I can't make it myself. There is no way for me to get to heaven except God's way." You then become a Christian, a part of God's forever family by accepting Christ. And Jesus Christ comes to dwell in your life, as He has in the lives of the athletes in this book, giving you the same kind of power He has given these men.

If you say *no*,

you reject Him. You condemn Him as a psychotic—as one who was probably insane, daring to say He was the only way to heaven.

If you say *maybe*,

you play with the X factor of death in your life, because our maybe becomes an automatic no if we should die.

Simply, it boils down to this.

First: God's game plan is to face the fact that we're separated from God by our sin and that there is no way we, by ourselves, can reach God.

Second: God gave an answer in His Son, Jesus Christ—the only answer available to us.

Third: We have to make a decision. We must say yes or no to Him. The choice is up to us. God has done His thing. He sent His Son to the cross for us. Now it is up to us. I hope and pray, if you personally have not asked Christ to become your Saviour, that you will do this very simply with a prayer like this:

Dear God, I realize I am a sinner. I realize that Jesus Christ, Your Son, came to die on the cross, to be buried, and to rise again from the dead. Forgive my sins.

I personally accept Jesus Christ, Your Son, into my heart as my own personal Saviour now.

Thank You for letting me become a child of Yours and for allowing me to become a part of Your forever family.

In Jesus' Name, AMEN.

After you have made this decision,

Let God's Word, His rule book, be your guide as you play the game of life for keeps.

Let this be your goal.

Let this be your Supergoal!